Planning For Reading Success

Book 2: Reading: Teaching for learning

Vera Southgate

Planning For Reading Success

Book 2:
Reading: Teaching for learning

Vera Southgate

Macmillan Education

First published 1984

Published by
MACMILLAN EDUCATION LTD
London and Basingstoke
Associated companies and representatives
throughout the world

ISBN 0 333 34695 5 HC
ISBN 0 333 34696 3 Ppr

Typeset by Acorn Origination, Bournemouth

Printed in Hong Kong

Contents

Acknowledgements

The author and publishers wish to thank the following who have kindly given permission for the use of copyright material:

Cambridge University Press for an extract from *Reading* by F Smith (1978).

The Controller of Her Majesty's Office for extracts from *The Bullock Report*, (1975).

Heinemann Educational Books for an extract from Schools Council: *Extending Beginning Reading* by V Southgate, H Arnold and S Johnson.

Every effort has been made to trace all the copyright holders but if any have been inadvertently overlooked the publishers will be pleased to make the necessary arrangements at the first opportunity.

Preface

This book is the second in a series of three books planned for teachers, under the overall title of *Planning For Reading Success*. The series has been designed to provide practical help for teachers and students in their continual search for ways of improving their techniques for helping their pupils, not only to enjoy reading, but also to read more effectively. These are essentially simple books and, I hope, practical ones. They do not demand the purchase of large quantities of new books or equipment. Indeed, as is pointed out, many of the solutions to the question of helping children to read are already to hand in the schools. Consequently, many ways are suggested of how full discussions, definitions of desired goals, imaginative and detailed planning for the use of available resources and the sharing of tasks among all the interested parties – teachers, students, parents, pupils, as well as friends and relatives – can completely revitalise reading within any school, almost regardless of the ages of its pupils.

In Book 1, *Children who do read*, practical suggestions are put forward for ensuring that all children learn to enjoy reading by being encouraged to read, for themselves, large numbers of books they have personally selected, from collections of books which their teachers know that they will be able to read.

Once this first step of reading for pleasure has been established, teachers will still want to know when and how their own teaching skills should be brought into action. Accordingly, Book 2, *Reading: Teaching for learning*, is concerned with those skills which can benefit from small amounts of direct teaching. Even more important, practical suggestions are made of how teachers can provide appropriate practices to ensure that the skills taught have been learned, and can check on what has and has not been mastered, in order that further guided practice can be arranged when necessary.

Finally, Book 3, *Reading for information*, provides simple information about study skills, together with definite details of methods whereby teachers can begin to extend their pupils proficiencies in this essential, but frequently neglected, area of reading competency.

April 1982   Vera Southgate

PART ONE

Teaching, Reading and Learning to Read

Chapter 1

Learning related to teaching

I Introduction

This particular book for teachers is the second in a series entitled *Planning For Reading Success*. In the first book *Children who do read* (Southgate, 1983), the emphasis was on the importance of teachers ensuring that their pupils, from a very early stage, were encouraged to read personally selected books, for their own pleasure and information. Suggestions were made about guiding children to choose books which were within their capabilities, and for providing opportunities for uninterrupted, silent reading. Various ways of promoting children's interest in books were also described. It was stated that if these measures were taken, all children would be likely to make better progress than has frequently been the case and that nearly all children could become successful readers, albeit at different levels.

The question was then put forward of whether this was *all* that teachers needed to do. The answer given was that certain amounts of direct teaching were also necessary in order that children would be helped to master specific skills. It was also indicated that this particular aspect of the teaching-learning process would be considered in this second book in the series.

II Principles for effective teaching and learning

A The relationship between teaching and learning

The aim of all teaching is that learning should take place. An obvious statement, you may think. Yet I have frequently observed that teachers, in their eagerness to ensure that their pupils do learn to read, often appear to concentrate more on what they should teach and how they should teach it, than on questions relating to how children do learn, and whether or not individual children have actually learned what they themselves have been so earnestly trying to teach. The result of teachers' concentration on their own very great efforts is that frequently insufficient time is left to consider ways in which effective learning can be encouraged, and also to check whether the expected learning has actually taken place.

The relationship between teaching and learning was spelt out very clearly over thirty years ago by Anderson and Dearbon *(The Psychology of Teaching, Reading, 1952)* when they stated, 'The teaching process must take its cue from the learning process.' Accordingly, in order to appreciate what the effective teacher needs to do, to ensure that learning does take place, let us first consider a little of what we know about how children learn.

B   General requisites for successful learning

The field of educational psychology provides us with various theories of learning, of which probably the two most important are, historically: first, the stimulus response theory and, secondly, the Gestalt theory, with its emphasis on problem solving and insight. Both theories have implications for learning to read and, consequently for teaching reading. However, as this is not in any way a theoretical book, but rather an attempt to provide teachers with a certain amount of practical guidance for helping children to learn to read, that is ideas and techniques which I have personally found to be effective or which I have observed teachers using successfully, the implications will be presented incidentally rather than specifically.

All that needs to be stated at this point is that a child is most likely to learn to read effectively, and with pleasure, if the following conditions exist.

1 He★ is strongly motivated, i.e. he *wants* to learn to read and to improve his reading performance. (If he has already been introduced to a graded collection of books and given adequate opportunities for reading personally chosen books at an appropriate level, as suggested in Book 1 of this series – *Children who do read* (Southgate, 1983) – he *will* be strongly motivated to increase his proficiency.)

2 He has been guided by his teacher to reading activities which are within his capabilities, and the steps forward in the learning process have been so minutely graded that none of them presented the child with what might have appeared to him to be an unsurmountable objective.

3 The learning tasks set before him have been so structured that he has been guided to 'insightful' learning.

★N.B. To avoid the clumsy usage of he/she and him/her, throughout this book the convention is followed of referring to the teacher as female and the pupils as male.

4   His acquisition of skills at every stage has been reinforced, by his teacher confirming that his responses were correct and praising his success – thus ensuring that his motivation has remained high.

5   He has been provided with appropriate and interesting activities for practising each newly acquired skill, so that each is totally mastered.

6   The child's continuing success will have led him to conceive for himself ever higher 'levels of aspiration'. In other words, the engineering of success for him, by his teacher, will have ensured that he is eager to go on improving his own performance.

C   General facets of successful teaching

The foregoing requisites for successful learning have inevitably highlighted certain of the major components of successful teaching. Thus the successful teacher of reading will endeavour to ensure that her pupils are highly motivated, and that each step forward is gradual and is geared to the child's capabilities. She will provide appropriate and stimulating activities for practice at each stage and will praise the success which inevitably follows. In addition to these facets of good teaching, there are three further activities in which the effective teacher of reading will be continuously engaged.

First, she will always need to check, for every child, whether or not each piece of teaching, guidance and practice has resulted in successful learning. This seems an obvious step to take, yet it is noticeable that a devoted teacher is frequently so busy organising learning situations or listening to children's individual oral reading that she quite often fails to check whether or not each child concerned has effectively learned what she is working so hard to teach him. Yet, what a waste of all the teacher's efforts if she does not make time for this checking, which should form an integral part of her teaching–learning plans! If a teacher fails in this vital aspect of her work, it is inevitable that she will either proceed to dissipate her energies, and the child's time, by going over things which a proportion of her class have already mastered or, alternatively, try to teach certain children the succeeding step before they have mastered the preceding one.

Secondly, the results of the teacher's checks on whether particular pieces of teaching and guidance have resulted in successful learning, on the part of individual children, need to be recorded. Even more important, items which have *not* been mastered need to be specially noted. This process of effective diagnosis, that is of checking and recording, is one of the hall-marks of good teaching, as that which has not been successfully learned must form the core of the next teaching-learning programme for the child in question.

Consequently, the third activity in which the effective teacher will be engaged is planning, either an extension of the original teaching, or special training activities for those children who need further reinforcement of the skill in question. This will need to be followed by additional, and prefer-ably *different* activities, which will provide appropriate practice to make certain that that particular piece of learning does take place. It follows that further checks will be required until the teacher is satisfied that absolute success has been achieved.

Throughout this book, many examples are provided of both teaching and learning activities designed to result in effective learning on the part of pupils. In all the suggestions made, it is assumed that the teacher's role is that of a tutor rather than of a didactic teacher. A tutor's attention is usually concentrated more on the learner and on the learning process than on the actual teaching. It is for this reason that I tend to use the word 'tuition' to represent the dual role of the teacher – her concern being not merely that of imparting information and setting tasks, but being equally focused on the results of these efforts, in terms of effective pupil learning.

III   Specific skills involved in learning to read and in teaching reading

A   Requisite skills for effective reading

At any level of reading, providing that the reader is motivated to want to read, there are two main requisites before effective reading can take place. They are:

1   The reader must be able to identify, on sight, the major proportion of the words in the text;
2   The reader must have one, or preferably more than one, technique to help him to decipher those words in the text which he does not immediately recognise.

It also facilitates the process of reading, that is of understanding the message which underlies the words, if the reader has some background knowledge relating to the passage he is attempting to read.

1   Sight vocabulary

The desirable proportion of words in the text, of which the reader must have immediate recognition, is generally agreed to be between 95 and 99 per cent. When considering children, and especially younger pupils who are still in the early stages of learning to read, the latter figure would be the most appropriate for any reading material which the child was attempting to read without help from his teacher. (See Chapter 6 of *Children who do read* for further details of appropriate levels of difficulty of reading mate-rials.)

2 *Techniques for deciphering unknown words*

Until fairly recently, teachers tended to assume that the most important, and frequently indeed the only, tactic necessary for deciphering unknown words was the application of phonic rules. Consequently, an infant teacher listening to a child reading aloud, when the child came to a word he could not recognise, almost invariably used to say, 'Sound it out.' Even children aged 7 to 9+, in the Schools Council project: *Extending Beginning Reading* (Southgate *et all.*, 1981), when asked in individual interviews what they did when they came to a word which they did not know, usually said they tried to 'sound it out'. They had clearly been trained to believe that this was the correct tactic to use. 'Guessing' was something which had been frowned on.

Currently, however, many teachers are beginning to be aware that the effective reader uses a wider range of tactics to help him to 'read' unfamiliar words. He uses the clues provided by the passage itself. His awareness of the meaning of what he is reading provides him with 'semantic cues' to unknown words. His general awareness of the grammatical structure of our language provides him with 'syntactic cues' to help him to understand words he may at first sight be unable to decipher. When his phonic skills are also brought into action, along with the other two types of cues, the child may well be able to gain meaning from the word which at first glance caused him difficulty.

For this reason, when a teacher is listening to a child reading aloud to her and the child hesitates at an unfamiliar word, the teacher should encourage him to 'guess' what the word might be in the context of the sentence and paragraph he is reading. When a child fails to read a word, 'What to you think it might be?', could well be a more helpful preliminary response from the teacher than the more usual, 'Sound it out.' When the child has 'guessed' what the word might be likely to be, if it is to make sense in the context of what he is reading, his knowledge of phonics can *then* be brought into play, to confirm or refute his initial attempt at the word. At that stage, if the child in using the phonic cues produces an incorrect word, he can be asked to read the sentence again to see if the suggested word does make sense.

The teacher's efforts to encourage the child to utilise the meaning of the passage to help him to read new words, rather than always concentrating on phonics, as a first line of attack, will be helpful to him in another way. One of the teacher's long-term objectives for her pupils is that they will become fluent readers. The fluent reader moves his eyes quickly along the lines of print, making sense of the text, with as few halts as possible. To encourage a child to stop at every word about which he is uncertain and then to endeavour laboriously to puzzle it out, is to set up a pattern of automatic and often lengthy halts. Such a procedure is the exact opposite of the fluent, meaningful reading which should be the teacher's chief objective for each pupil.

3   *Continually expanding vocabulary*

One further point needs to be borne in mind about the child's ever-increasing sight vocabulary. Not only does the effective reader need to have a large sight vocabulary of words which he can pronounce, but he must also be aware of their meanings. Consequently, a continually expanding knowledge of the meanings of words is also essential – and for many children this will not occur by chance. The teacher will need to be constantly engineering situations and activities for ensuring that vocabulary extension is taking place.

4   *General comprehension*

Even so, a sight vocabulary of discrete words, a familiarity with phonic rules and a growing knowledge of the meanings of words and phrases are only three of the elements to be utilised in the most important, and indeed the ultimate skill of reading, that is global comprehension of passages of increasing length – sentences, paragraphs, chapters and eventually whole books. This global comprehension is achieved most easily when the reader has some familiarity with the background against which the text is set.

B   Requisite skills for the teacher of reading

In order to provide appropriate tuition, designed to forward all her pupils' reading progress and help them to become habitual readers, what does a teacher of reading need to know and to do?

1   *The teacher as a reader*

The first requisite is that every teacher, regardless of the ages of the pupils in her class, needs to be convinced of the importance of learning to read and the pleasures which reading can provide – in other words, teachers themselves should be real readers.

2   *Teachers' background knowledge*

Teachers need to be knowledgeable about the many skills which are utilised in the complex, global act of reading. This background knowledge of the processes of learning to read, and of using one's reading skills for different purposes, needs to be sufficiently broad to encompass all the diverse levels of reading abilities of the pupils in a teacher's class. Indeed, her expertise needs to extend beyond the level of the best reader in the class, otherwise how can she make effective plans for forwarding the reading progress of her most advanced pupils?

It follows that a teacher's own knowledge about reading can only be applied effectively to help all her pupils, if she is aware of the widely different levels of reading attainment within her class. The range of reading abilities in any class is quite frequently much wider than teachers who have not checked this might imagine. For example, it is not unusual to find, in a class made up of any age-group of children from 7 year olds to 11 year olds, a range of reading abilities which extend from beginning reading to a Reading Age of 14 years or so.

Teachers cannot be aware of their pupils' general levels of reading abilities unless they have tested them. As group tests of reading are acceptable for establishing general levels of reading ability, teachers' background knowledge must also include an awareness of the usefulness of available group reading tests.

3 Diagnostic knowledge of children's strengths and weaknesses

Thirdly, the teacher needs, not only to know children's general level of reading ability, but she also requires a detailed, ongoing knowledge of each pupil's strengths and weaknesses. For example, to plan adequate, appropriate tuition for every pupil, the teacher needs to be aware of:

(a) His sight vocabulary and, more particularly, the most commonly used words in our language which he fails to recognise instantly – for example, those he fails to recognise in the first 200 words of *Key Words to Literacy* (McNally and Murray, 1962);
(b) His mastery of phonic rules and, again, especially his weaknesses;
(c) The extent of his knowledge of the meanings of words;
(d) His strengths and weaknesses in using the semantic and syntactic cues of the text;
(e) His ability to grasp the meaning of sentences, paragraphs and more extensive passages of prose, i.e. his comprehension;
(f) And, finally, although by no means the least important, any particular interest or interests which he may have.

This diagnostic knowledge on the part of the teacher, of course, demands not only an awareness of a variety of individual assessment techniques but also the development of a habit of meticulous record-keeping for each child. This can include the child's own records, as well as the teacher's personal records.

4 Teaching and learning techniques

Teachers certainly need to be able to draw on a variety of teaching techniques but, even more important, they must have available a wide repertoire of activities designed to provide their pupils with interesting and enjoyable practice in the skills being taught – practice designed to ensure that learning does actually take place.

If teachers are uncertain about their knowledge in any of these spheres, there is no longer a dearth of books from which they can gather knowledge about the reading process and about techniques for providing children with guided practice. In addition, in Chapters 3 and 4 of this book, many activities are described which will provide children with practice for consolidating their growing skill in the speedy recognition of sight words.

5   Knowledge of reading resources

Every teacher also requires a wide acquaintance with all the available reading resources which can help her to forward her pupils' reading progress. This means not only the 'teaching books' on which she might base her reading teaching, but also all the teaching aids which can help to reinforce her teaching, as well as provide her pupils with the necessary and valuable practice to ensure that what has been taught is effectively learned. It is also important that the teacher is familiar with the fiction and non-fiction books available to and suitable for her pupils. This implies that teachers should have actually read all or the majority of such books, as opposed merely to glancing at them. (It is suggested in *Children who do read* (Southgate, 1983) that some of teachers' personal reading of children's books might be undertaken on the occasions when their pupils are engaged in their own personal reading.)

IV   Conclusions

It can easily be appreciated from the preceding lists that to be a good teacher of reading is not a simple matter; the task makes great demands on the teacher's expertise, time and energy. Not all teachers have the required expertise – particularly those whose training occurred before the publication of the Bullock Report, *A Language for Life* (Department of Education and Science, 1975) – and before the setting up of courses of advanced training in reading and the language arts at the Open University and other Universities and Colleges of Higher Education.

While a large proportion of school time is usually set aside in primary schools for the teaching of reading and related subjects, and teachers certainly devote a great deal of energy to trying to forward their pupils' reading progress, this time and energy is not always employed in ways likely to achieve the optimum result. For example, in *Extending Beginning Reading* (op. cit.) it was found that the time set aside for reading tuition by teachers of children aged 7 to 9+ was mainly utilised for listening to individual children's oral reading. In such periods the teachers worked extremely hard, constantly switching their attention from the child who was reading aloud to other children in the classroom, with the result that the total time devoted to any one child only averaged out at thirty seconds. This time was clearly totally inadequate for diagnosing a child's weaknesses, introducing him to appropriate practice activities, probing his comprehension of the passage read or discussing his interests.

In fact, it is clear that many teachers not only need, but are also eager to acquire, more knowledge about reading. It is also clear that the use of their own time and their pupils' time frequently requires a complete reorganisation. It is not sufficient that teachers themselves should work very hard – which they do – it is even more important that their efforts should be effective, in terms of their pupils' learning and their attitudes to reading.

In the remainder of this book, teachers will find many practical suggestions relating to what needs to be taught and details of activities which will ensure that learning does take place, as well as methods of assessing and recording progress. Finally, in Chapter 7, the question of the organisation of the varied teaching and learning activities is explored and specific suggestions put forward to ensure that the very great efforts which teachers undoubtedly do make might be channelled into more effective reading programmes.

As almost the whole of this book is concerned with teaching and learning activities, a word of warning would seem appropriate. As stated in *Children who do read* (Southgate, 1983), I firmly believe that the major portion of any reading programme should consist of children's private reading of books which they have personally selected from a graded collection of books, at levels which their teacher knows they will be able to read. The teacher–learning activities suggested in this book should form the minor, rather than the major, proportion of a well-balanced programme of reading tuition.

Chapter 2

A systematic plan for teaching and learning sight words

I Planning for effective learning of sight words

It has been suggested in Chapter 1 that, if a child is to be able to read continuous prose with understanding, the first requisite is that he needs to recognise instantly, on sight, approximately 99 per cent of the words in the text. To 'recognise', in this context, means to be able, not just to pronounce the word, but even more important, to understand its meaning. It follows that the teacher of reading, at every level, must be consciously and continually working towards enlarging each child's sight vocabulary. This objective is unlikely to be achieved unless the teacher formulates specific and systematic plans for ensuring that this vital part of learning forms a continuous process for each pupil.

An outline plan for an effective pattern of teaching and practice activities, designed to ensure that every child begins to gain instant recognition of the particular words his teacher wishes him to learn or he himself wants to learn, could be based on the following steps.

1   The teacher introduces a small number of 'interesting' words to either a group of children or, occasionally, the whole class. The words will not be merely a group of words which the teacher thinks the children ought to learn. On the contrary, they will be words in a particular context – something in which the children are currently interested, such as the shop or post office within the classroom or school, a school outing or concert, the approach of Christmas or the summer holidays, some subject in which they have a particular interest, such as tadpoles and frogs, spring bulbs, old castles, Eskimos or dinosaurs. Noteworthy national or local events in which the whole class are interested also stimulate the need to learn to read new words. These words will have arisen naturally in activities and discussions among the children and between the teacher and children and, consequently, the children will know what the words mean and will be interested in them. They will

want to be able to read them on labels and notices, as well as to use them in their own writing.

2 The teacher will introduce a small number of these selected words, printed on large flash-cards, to the group of children concerned and do a small amount of direct teaching.

3 This first step is reinforced by teacher-directed practice using the large flash-cards and, later, perhaps some form of tachistoscope (see page 16).

4 Teacher-directed activities, most probably in the form of games, are introduced in order to reinforce the learning and to accelerate the speed of word recognition.

5 Group games which do not require the teacher's supervision are introduced to provide further reinforcement of the learning process and to accelerate the speed of recognition of the words.

6 Activities for individual practice, including a procedure for re-learning are introduced.

7 The procedures for individual practice are accompanied by a related system of checking and recording.

II Teaching activities

A Size and composition of teaching group

Although there may, on certain occasions, have been a class session on introducing children to new words relating to a special subject or occasion in which they were all interested, learning to recognise these words is unlikely to be a class activity. In every class it is usual to find pupils of widely divergent reading standards and, consequently, very different levels of sight vocabulary. Many of the children in the class may well learn to recognise the new words in a matter of minutes. Other children will require specific practice.

Accordingly, the preliminary stages of teaching new sight words will generally involve only a small group of children – probably no more than five or six children, who do *not* quickly recognise the words to be practised. Frequent checking of individual children in the group will ensure that as soon as any child can recognise all the words with speed, he will be given practice in recognising another set of flash-cards. It follows that, as not all children in the group will achieve speedy recognition of a particular group of words at the same time, such groups must be *ad hoc* rather than permanent or semi-permanent groups.

B Introduction of new sight words

There has been a good deal of research into the two questions of whether children should be taught sight words in context or in isolation, and also whether or not each sight word should be accompanied by an illustration – where this is possible. (See, for example, Ceprano, M. A. (1981) 'A review of selected research on methods of teaching sight words'.) The evidence is frequently conflicting, depending largely on the designs of the experiments. One pointer which does emerge from the results, however, is that when a teacher chooses a collection of discrete words to be taught, it is helpful to ensure that the words differ in length, shape and letter characteristics, and for the teacher to draw children's attention to these differences as each word is introduced.

There are also indications in the research findings that when a word or a sentence is introduced alongside an illustration, it cannot be assumed that the child's attention will be focused on the details of the word rather than on the picture, unless the teacher specifically guides her pupils' attention to the characteristic details of each word.

The direct teaching of new sight words will involve the teacher in showing the word on a flash-card and/or writing it on a blackboard, pronouncing it and discussing its meaning with the children – where this is possible. When the words do not have interesting meanings in isolation, as for example, 'in', 'on', 'under', 'front' or 'behind', they can be introduced in spoken sentences and illustrated by placing a box on a table, together with a small toy which can be moved to various positions relative to the box. Certain verbs, such as 'stand', 'sit', 'walk' and 'smile', can sometimes be introduced by having children perform the actions.

The large flash-cards which the teacher will generally use for introducing new sight words (or phrases or sentences) can be either hand-made or commercially produced. In the latter case, the pack of such cards is usually intended as an adjunct to a reading scheme. Alternatively, or in addition, the teacher may produce her own flash-cards. In the latter event, the flash-cards for single words, which should be made of fairly stiff white or light-coloured card, should be approximately 25 cm by 10 cm. The cards should *all* be sufficiently long to accommodate the longest word the children are likely to be asked to learn. If this is not done, and the word 'a', for example, is printed on a short card and the word 'elephant' on a long card, a child may well use the length of the cards as clues, instead of the total shape of the word and/or the arrangement of letters of which the word consists. The printing of the words is usually done with a black thick-tipped felt pen, and the letters should be sufficiently bold and clear for a small group of children to be able to see them without strain.

C   Training in rapid word recognition

Once the group of children can recognise the small batch of words which the teacher is currently trying to teach them, the second and most important stage is to speed up their rate of recognition. This is a crucial stage, as fluent reading depends on the speed with which the reader's eyes move along the lines of print. Gaining meaning from the text is partly a result of this rapid recognition of words. When a child has to halt or hesitate at individual words, this impedes the process of understanding the meaning of the text he is trying to read. Consequently, if the teacher continues to expose a flash-card for too long a period, the child will be able to have two or three eyes fixations or even try to puzzle out the word with the help of phonics. This is not the aim of the activity: the objective is to encourage *instant* recognition. The teacher's first objective should be to expose each word for only a second, and later speed this up even further, in order that the children will eventually be trained to recognise the word with only one eye fixation. In this context it is useful to bear in mind that the average duration of each eye fixation for fluent adult readers is about one quarter of a second.

Of course, this training in rapid recognition of discrete words will occupy only a very small proportion of the time devoted to teaching, practising and learning to read. It is, however, worth mentioning at this point that, for children to have access to books sufficiently easy for them to read without having to hesitate at unfamiliar words, does encourage and help to establish rapid eye movements along lines of continuous prose.

D Methods of exposing flash-cards

The two main methods which a teacher can use to expose flash-cards to children at regular and increasingly brief intervals are to manipulate the cards manually or to use some form of tachistoscope.

1 Manual manipulation

For the teacher to achieve a regularly and appropriately timed rhythm for exposing a set of flash-cards to a group of children will take a little practice. To sit at a table is usually easier than standing, as the bottom edges of the pack of cards can be rested on the table. Some teachers find it helpful to use a blank card to cover the pack of word cards and then to remove it for only a second before it is replaced. Until the children are used to the procedure, the number of flash-cards in a pack should be small, perhaps no more than six or eight cards at first. The time spent on this activity should also be very brief.

2 Tachistoscopes

A tachistoscope is a device which allows visual material, for example a series of pictures or words, to be presented at very brief, regularly timed intervals. In the 1939–45 war, such machines proved valuable for training observers in the rapid identification of different types of aeroplanes. Since then, many specialised projectors have been commercially produced and used, particularly in the USA, not only to teach speedy recognition of individual words, but also to increase the speed of adults' reading.

At a simpler level, slide or film projectors can be used for increasing the speed of recognition of discrete words, as can simple hand-made tachistoscopes. Harris and Sipay (*How to Increase Reading Ability*, 1975) provide an illustration of a hand-made model in stiff cardboard, which rests on a table and is operated by the teacher, who is standing or sitting behind the table.

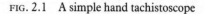

FIG. 2.1   A simple hand tachistoscope

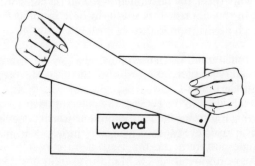

The words to be printed on the flash-cards should be in such a position that when any card is placed with its lower edge on the table, the word will appear in the aperture on the screen. Teachers with an inventive turn of mind can, no doubt, devise alternative simple forms of hand-made tachistoscopes.

III   Activities for providing practice

For effective learning of sight words to take place, the teacher-directed activity of using large flash-cards with a small group of children needs to be followed by practice activities on the part of the children concerned. The most effective practice activities may be described as those which place the child in a position in which he is required to make a verbal or other response to the written symbol of a particular word – a response which will indicate that he can pronounce and/or knows the meaning of the word in question. The teacher who has used a number of large flash-cards with a group of children, after eliciting communal responses from the group, usually asks individual children to pronounce particular words. Fortunately, there are many additional games which children will enjoy playing and which will also achieve the same end of revealing whether or not an individual child can pronounce a word and/or understand its meaning.

A   Matching activities

A preliminary activity involves the matching of identical words. For example, suppose that there is a shop in the classroom and the teacher has used, with a group of children, a pack of large flash-cards made up of words relating to articles in the shop. The teacher and the group can then go to the shop and match the large flash-cards to smaller cards which are displayed alongside the articles in the shop. Children can next do this matching in pairs and eventually on their own. It should be noted that such an exercise is rarely merely 'matching', as it would be if two unidentifiable shapes were being matched. The word on the large flash-card, when placed beside the small card attached to the object in the shop is not just a shape to the child – a shape matching another identical shape. It has meaning for him. He knows that the black letters on both cards say 'chocolate', for example. The written symbols thus have meaning for him. The learning can be reinforced by asking him to say the word as he places one card beside the other.

The children's learning of these particular words can be further reinforced by playing a simple matching game with small cards 10 cm by 5 cm. These should be made of stiff card with the words clearly printed in black. A small triangle cut from the top right-hand corner of each card will ensure that the words are always held in the upright position and simplify correct stacking.

Game 1: Pairs

This game can be played by two children, both sitting at the same side of a table or desk. Two small packs of identical cards of words which are currently being practised are required for this game. The two packs of cards are shuffled and spread out face upwards in random order on the table or desk. The cards should be placed in such a way that the words are parallel to the children, so that they are at the correct angles for reading the words. Each child then takes it in turn to try to point to two identical cards and name them. If the cards selected are not identical, or if the child cannot pronounce them correctly, they must be left on the table. If the child's response is correct, he picks up the pair of cards. When all the cards have been removed from the table, the child with the most pairs of words is the winner. As a small group activity, for between two and four children, this is best directed by the teacher in the first instance, as she can check that the children are able to read the words they have selected. The game also offers a further opportunity for teaching, in that the teacher can point out differences in letters in similar, but not identical words which have been mismatched. Although this is an activity of particular value in the early stages of reading, when the pairs of words can be of different lengths and shapes, it is also of use at a later stage when words of very similar overall appearance can be used. At that point, the game can also be used to help children to practise phonic rules.

For children to be able to play this game on their own, it will be necessary to have small pictures of the objects in question on the back of the cards. For example, if this is a follow-up activity to the teacher's presentation of large flash-cards relating to objects in the shop, such as chocolates, cake, biscuits and tea, these objects would be depicted on the reverse sides of the appropriate cards. In that event, after a player had pointed to two identical words and named them, the cards would be reversed to expose the pictures, thus providing indisputable proof of the correctness or otherwise of his response.

B   Group games – in general

Group activities in which children can be engaged, as a means of practising quick recognition of sight words, usually take the form of simple competitive games. Consequently, they represent, for the children, a most enjoyable activity, and for the teacher an effective means of reinforcing the children's learning.

The cards used in such games should be of similar size to those just described in 'pairs'. The packs of cards may be groups of 'Key Words to Literacy' (see Chapter 4), the names of children in the class, a group of words, such as 'animals' or 'games', or any other set of words in which the class is currently interested and/or the teacher wants the children to learn as sight words. The number of cards in each pack will depend on the stage of progress the children have reached, and also on the number of children likely to be involved in playing any game. The smaller the group, the more 'turns' each child will have, and thus the more attentive he will be, and this will result in more learning taking place. If the group is too large, the children will lose interest, behaviour problems will arise and learning will decrease. For certain games two children are ideal, when 10–16 words could be used. For many other games four children would form a convenient group, and in that case 16–24 words in a pack would probably be appropriate, although the number of cards may later be increased.

The group engaged in any game should, of course, consist only of children who actually need practice in particular groups of words which have recently been introduced. If children *can* read these sight words with speed, there is no reason for arranging for them to play such games with that particular pack of cards. This means that the teacher needs to be continually checking – a point discussed later in this chapter. When an individual child knows the words, fresh words need to be introduced and then used for practice in the same game or in a different game. The most popular games can be reserved for the dullest words, for example, 'and', 'the', 'that' or 'was' – four of the most commonly used words in the English language, as listed in *Key Words to Literacy* (McNally & Murray, 1962).

C Self-checking devices

The small cards used in many of the group games and individual activities in which children will be engaged as they practise quick recognition of new words need, whenever possible, to have checking devices on their reverse sides. Of course, this is not always possible, as many of the most frequently used words in our language do not lend themselves to pictorial representation. Many nouns, however, can be represented by pictures, diagrams, or other illustrations, as suggested for the game of 'Pairs'. Small pictures cut out of comics, newspapers or magazines can be stuck onto the reverse sides of the cards. The pictures or diagrams should always be as simple as possible, with all irrelevancies and background details eliminated. For example, a cow should not be shown against the background of a field or farm, while a house should just be a stylised house with no garden. A box can be kept in the classroom of small illustrations which might be useful. Both children and parents can contribute to this collection. Certain publishers also produce small pictures for this purpose. Pin-men can sometimes be used to illustrate verbs. Colours, shapes and numbers also lend themselves easily to checking symbols. All such cards provide the opportunity for children to play many practice games in groups, or to engage in individual practice activities, without continual supervision.

D Grouping and storing flash-cards

The teacher will find it helpful to write a code reference, for example a letter and a number, on the back of each card. Each group of cards can then be held together with a rubber band and they can be stacked, in order, in a box of appropriate size. These same code references will also need to be printed on the reverse sides of the small flash-cards which children will later use in individual practice and in group games. The code reference numbers are essential for ensuring that cards belonging to a particular group or game are collected and store appropriately. They also form a means of identifying cards which may have been dropped and then found later. Each small pack of individual cards is best stored in its own small cardboard or metal box. There should be a label on the outside of each box, for example, 'Colours', 'Numbers', 'Animals' or 'People', as well as the reference number of the particular set of cards. These small boxes can be kept in larger boxes of the appropriate size, for example shoe boxes. If the small boxes are stood on their sides, so that the labels on the lids are facing the front, children will soon learn to recognise the composite word which distinguishes a group of words of a particular class. Many helpful suggestions on the indentification and storage of cards and other forms of apparatus used in games can be found in *40 Reading Games to Make and Play* (Root, 1982).

E   Help with preparing cards

The making of large and small flash-cards, and the collection of small pictures to illustrate words can be an extremely time-consuming business. Consequently teachers, working on the principle that their own time will be most profitably spent on the skilled activities which they are best qualified to undertake, would be well advised to delegate, wherever possible, the preparation of cards and games to other people. The children themselves will enjoy collecting pictures of the appropriate size from comics, magazines and newspapers. Parents, coming to school for, say, one half-day a week, will also be willing to help in the preparation of cards and games.

F   Extension of practice activities

This particular chapter should be regarded merely as a brief general introduction to a systematic plan for ensuring a continuing expansion of each child's sight vocabulary. In later chapters detailed descriptions are provided of many games and activities, aimed at helping children's speedy recognition of an increasing number of words. Many of these activities, including class and group games, as well as individual activities, can equally well be used for teaching and practising phonic rules. In each of these categories, methods of checking and recording children's progress are expanded, so that re-learning activities may be introduced or progressive programmes of new learning be put into effect for groups of children or for individuals.

IV   Checking and recording

If a teacher accepts that for only a very small proportion of her time will the ongoing teaching–learning activities involve the whole class, it follows that the majority of the teaching–learning programme will involve group activities and individual activities. This is a complicated task to organise and there is no way in which it can be accomplished effectively unless a well-planned system of checking and recording is in force.

Planning graded steps forward for every pupil first involves subdividing the task into small manageable units. The example already given of the words referring to the names of objects in the shop, will provide a useful example. There may be as many as 50 or 100 different objects in a shop or post office, but very young children may, at first, only be able to cope with learning as sight words ten of these words. In that event, the first group of words to be practised in this category would only comprise ten cards. Later the number of cards could be raised to 15–20. The labels on the small boxes of cards should indicate this fact by, for instance, Shop 1–15 or Shop 16–30. The reference on the back of each card could then be the word 'Shop' or an abbreviation, followed by the actual number of the card. At a slightly later stage, when the children are practising 'Key Words to Literacy', the reference numbers could follow those suggested on the record sheet in Appendix 3, e.g. KWL–1 or KWL–3 (b).

The teacher will then be in a position to keep absolutely accurate records of every child's success, so that each step mastered can be followed by planned activities and games related to the next stage in the reading programme. To achieve this, the teacher needs a record-card or sheet for each child or, preferably, a large book of squared paper. The left-hand page of the first double spread will contain a list of the children's names. The remaining pages of the book can be cut back to expose all the names. A horizontal line should then be drawn across the top of the pages with space above it for reference numbers, such as Sh/1–10 or KWL/21–40.

FIG. 2.2   A sample card

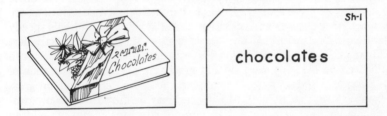

This makes record-keeping extremely simple. When it is thought that an individual child readily recognises a group of words or when, as will be suggested later, someone else has first checked his responses, he will come to his teacher for a final check. Suppose he only recognises 15 out of 20 words immediately, the teacher will pencil in the figure 15 in the appropriate square in her record-book. The child will be sent away to practise the five words he could not read. Alternatively, or in addition, he may also be included in a group game referring to this set of cards. Eventually, he will come back to the teacher for a further, final check of the whole group of cards. If all are correct, an ink tick can be made in place of the pencilled figure 15.

This kind of record-book provides the teacher with a complete picture of each child's mastery of sight words and also of gaps in his knowledge. In effect, it also shows exactly which children should be included in a particular *ad hoc* group to practise or re-learn particular groups of words.

PART TWO

Games and Activities for Enlarging Children's Sight Vocabularies

Chapter 3

Learning 'interesting' sight words

I 'Interesting' sight words first

Although *Key Words to Literacy* (McNally & Murray, 1962) are the most important words which children should be able to recognise instantly on sight, they are certainly not the first words which children should be taught. This is because only a minority of them are nouns and, consequently, the majority of the words have no intrinsic interest for children. They are mainly the 'carrier' or link words, which have little meaning on their own, although they do give active meaning to phrases, sentences and paragraphs. Consequently, a discussion of how these important words might be specifically learned and tested is deferred until Chapter 4, in order that various nouns and other words of more interest to children can be considered first.

II Suggestions for groups of words

A Children's names

With young children, in their first few months of attending school, the first sight words I should suggest helping each of them to recognise would be their own first names and then, gradually, the names of other children in the class. These are words of great personal interest to children. As soon as the child arrives at school on his first day, it is useful for the teacher to make a card for his desk or table by printing on it his first name and surname. Labels, also clearly printed, should be fixed to the peg where he is to hang his coat, any locker which he may be allocated, as well as any personal piece of equipment. Children of 6 years old and children in older classes and in remedial groups, who will have certain personal notebooks, such as 'My word book' (mentioned later), should also have their names printed on white labels attached to the fronts of the books. (Printed words on white gummed labels are much clearer for children to distinguish than names written on the covers of coloured notebooks). As other children will also have their own name-cards in front of them, a newcomer will soon learn to read the names of children sitting at his own table and of particular friends or other children sitting nearby. If there are children in the class with the same first name and the teacher introduces the newcomer to them and shows him their name-cards, he will soon learn to distinguish these cards by their surnames, in addition to their first names.

Gradually, the child will learn to recognise the first names of all the children in the class, through the many activities which can be organised using name-cards. For example, one simple activity is to have all the name-cards which are lying on desks or tables gathered in at the end of every afternoon by two selected children and distributed next morning by two different children. A newcomer helping a more experienced child in these activities will quickly learn to read the names of all the pupils in the class. The activity of different children being allocated to distribute notebooks, by reading correctly the name on each label, will also reinforce their recognition of each other's names. Rotas can be put up on a wall-chart for the collection and distribution of name-cards and of notebooks, as well as for other regular classroom jobs, and these will provide more practice in reading names, as well as helping children to learn to read the days of the week.

Spache (*Reading Activities for Child Involvement*, 1972) suggests an interesting activity using children's name-cards. She calls it the 'Roll Call' game and suggests that the children should have duplicated copies of their name-cards to put along the rail below the blackboard. On arrival every morning, each child should match his own name-card with the duplicated card on the rail and then drop the duplicate card into a box labelled: 'We are here'. Absent children can then be identified by the names remaining on the rail.

This idea could quite well be combined with an earlier suggestion, without having to duplicate names. The children's name-cards, which had been collected at the end of the previous afternoon, could be set out in random order on the rail or a window-sill or the teacher's table, by different children every morning. As the class come into the classroom each child could find his own card and drop it into the box. A rota of children could then distribute the cards from the box to the appropriate desks.

Name-cards for a class can be used for various sorting activities, for example into boys' names and girls' names. A reference list on the wall, showing the names in two columns, arranged in alphabetical order of first names could be referred to as a check when the sorting was complete. At a later stage, with older children, the list of names could be arranged in the normal adult manner, alphabetically in order of surnames. These same lists would then form a useful point of reference for learning at a later stage, the order of the letters of the alphabet – as outlined in Book 3 of this series, entitled *Reading for information*.

A further way of helping children to learn to read the names of all the children in their class is to prepare a large chart showing the layout of all the seating positions in the classroom. When in use, this chart can either be placed on a large table or on the floor. Two children working together can gather in the name-cards from the desks, and place each name on the appropriate oblong on the chart. When these are checked as correct by either a 'child-checker' (mentioned later) or the teacher, the pair can gather up the cards, halve them and then see who is first to distribute his share to the appropriate children's desks. This is also a useful device for older children, for example in the first few weeks of being promoted to a new school, such as a junior school or a middle school, or even for secondary school pupils joining a remedial class.

Many other ways of reinforcing the learning of the names can easily be organised. Lists of names on rotas on the wall, for example, of children who will look after the flowers in any week, of those who will tidy the book shelves or undertake other jobs, will all help to make the names familiar. Children's names on artwork or written work displayed on notice-boards or walls will soon begin to be recognised, as will such notices as 'Stephen Dodds brought these flowers', which are seen on many nature tables in infant classes.

B Additional interesting words, phrases and sentences

Even while children are learning to recognise the names of other pupils in the class, they will be beginning to recognise additional words of special interest to themselves and, at first, these will frequently be nouns. The words on cards, attached to many of the objects in infant classrooms are often among the first words which children learn to recognise in school, for example the pieces of furniture and equipment in the room – 'table', 'chair', 'desk', 'blackboard', 'books', 'paint', 'shop' and so on. However, to leave these cards permanently in place is not necessarily the best way of helping children to recognise the words. A system of children gathering in all the cards at intervals and redistributing them to the appropriate places would hasten the process of effective recognition.

Displays of all kinds, so frequently seen in first schools and primary schools, of flowers, toys, books, interesting and curious artefacts, as well as equipment in the form of a shop, post office or puppet theatre, boxes of junk, dressing-up clothes, sand trays, scales and weights, liquid measures, woodwork tools and cookery equipment, all make their contribution to the store of available, interesting words. In many of these cases the words on the attached notices take the form of phrases or sentences, which children soon learn to recognise. The sentences are particularly useful because, as well as including verbs and adjectives attached to the nouns which interest children, they also incorporate certain of the 'key words' which are so essential to their reading and which will later receive more specific teaching and practice. The speed of learning to recognise such phrases and sentences can be increased if the teacher prepares a duplicate of each notice, in the form of a large flash-card, to use in teaching-practice sessions, with groups of children; the teacher reading each sentence to the group, the group responding in unison and, later, individually, until familiarity brings an instant, correct response. This activity can be followed by practice for individuals or pairs of children, who will first try to read each sentence to himself or his partner, before going round the room to match the flash-cards to the sentences on display, as a means of checking the accuracy of their attempts.

The interaction between children's writing and reading also forwards the process of increasing children's sight vocabulary. The majority of teachers of younger children are well aware of this, so that displays of children's own written work and accounts of the many activities in which they are engaged are always on display in the schools, for other children to read. The key criteria in this respect are for the displays to look attractive and for them to be changed at frequent intervals. Such activities have been described in detail in many books for teachers, for example *Reading in the Modern Infants' School* (Goddard, 1969) and do not require enlarging here. The main point is to recognise the importance of making provision by activities and games for children's sight vocabulary of discrete words, phrases or sentences, to continue to increase, otherwise the initial interest in words and in reading may evaporate. As the Bullock Report, *A Language for Life* (D.E.S., 1975) stated:

> 'The major difficulty in maintaining this interest when they do come to read for themselves is that of building up, at a reasonable rate, the number of words they can recognise on sight.'

C   Other proper nouns

Even when children are able to read fairly fluently, say at the level of an average reader of 8 years, many still experience difficulty in reading proper nouns. For this reason, pupils should start to learn proper nouns as soon as possible. Once they can recognise the names of the pupils in their class, which for the majority of children will be before they are 6 years old, the teacher would be wise to introduce certain of the following categories of proper nouns.

1   The children's relatives

General words describing relatives, such as mother, Mummy, father, Daddy (including whatever the local variations of such words may be), brother, sister, aunt and auntie, grandmother, granny and so on, need to be discussed with the whole class and written on the blackboard. A permanent chart, headed 'Relatives' can be prepared and hung on the wall, as well as a box of small cards made for individual practice.

In addition, each child will require his own personal list of relatives on a card or in a notebook. He will then be able to consult this list for his free writing and so reinforce his recognition of more proper nouns. The following are examples of items in such a list.

My Dad, Daddy or father	– Mr William Green
(whichever word he personally uses)	
My sister	– Linda Green
My Uncle Bob	– Mr Robert Cox
My Auntie Jean	– Mrs Jean Bell

2 The names of teachers

Children can become familiar with the names of all the teachers in the school and other helpers, such as the caretaker and the dinner helpers, if a chart is prepared and, in a large school, perhaps a small box of cards. Some of the items on the chart might read as follows.

Mr Geoffrey Maddison	– Headteacher
Miss Lesley Smith	– Teacher of Class 1
Mrs Anne Atkinson	– Teacher of Class 2
Mr John Edwards	– Teacher of Class 3

If a box of small cards is prepared, the description of each person's job could appear on the reverse side of the card. For slower readers in a remedial group in a secondary school, the list would be much longer, of course.

3 Additional proper nouns

The following suggestions represent examples of additional proper nouns which children should be helped to recognise, on sight, by reference to lists and cards:

(a) The names of characters in current television programmes in which they are interested;
(b The names of characters in a book which the teacher is currently reading to them;
(c) Their own addresses;
(d) The correct name and address of the school;
(e) The name of the town or village in which they live, as well as the names of nearby towns, villages and counties;
(f) The names of certain countries and a few capital cities;
(g) The days of the week – the rhyme, 'Monday's child is fair of face', is useful for this purpose;
(h) The months of the year – the rhyme, 'January brings the snow', is useful here and can be followed by 'Thirty days hath September';
(i) The seasons of the year should be taught, although they are frequently written as common nouns, along with special festivals such as Christmas and Easter;

(j) Other words the children may see and which are generally written in block capitals, for example, POLICE, POST OFFICE, EXIT, ENTRANCE, CAR PARK, and the names of local shops and supermarkets, should also be learned by these various means.

The majority of these lists, for example the names of teachers in the school and the names of the days, months and seasons should be set out on wall-charts to which the children can have permanent access.

D   Special categories of words

Children's sight vocabulary of words which they find particularly interesting can very soon be extended to include learning to recognise words in special categories other than those already suggested. By so doing, children will be learning to *classify* words, which is one important part of vocabulary extension. Examples of such categories are: colours; numbers; animals; flowers; pets; people (i.e. teacher, doctor, dentist, nurse, etc.); toys; vehicles (i.e. car, bus, lorry, bicycle, etc.); food; clothes; and the seaside.

It will be noticed that nearly all these words are nouns which can easily be illustrated. 'Colours', of course, can also be easily illustrated by squares or circles of coloured gummed paper. Certain verbs, for example sit, stand, tie, run and jump, can be illustrated by pin-men. The fact that these words can be illustrated makes it easy to produce reference charts which children can consult when they are engaged in individual written work, and also to prepare boxes of small cards with reference checks on the reverse sides, which children can use for individual learning practice.

Those categories of words of particular interest to children at different times do not need to be learned in any special order. The time at which individual children or the whole class have a special current interest, will be the time when they are eager to take a box of small cards, practice reading them and then have their success checked off on their teacher's records. I have also known individual children, who had a special interest of their own, to come up with suggestions for categories of words in small boxes which they would like to help to make and which other children might also enjoy learning.

III   Practising word-recognition by playing group games

A   The value of group games

In the early stages of encouraging children's quick recognition of sight words, group games prove an enjoyable and effective means of practising speedy recognition of words. In the first instance, the small packs of cards to be used in such games should be those with self-checking devices on their reverse sides. The following suggestions represent only a small sample of games which will provide the necessary practice. In Appendix I a list of publications, describing a great variety of group activities and games, is provided.

B Order of play

In any group game, especially when children are to play it on their own, a quick method of deciding on the order of play should be established. This can be done either by throwing a die or, more quietly, by placing numbered counters of the same colour face down on a table, and shuffling them. The child choosing number one takes first turn.

C Examples of games

Game 2 (a): Pick a word

No. of players: Up to 4, but preferably 2
Equipment: Any pack of small cards (self-checking)
Method of play:
The cards are spread out in the centre of the table, with the words uppermost. The first child points to a word which he thinks he recognises and pronounces it. He then examines the checking device on the reverse of the card without exposing it to the other players. If he was correct, he exposes the reverse side and retains the card. If he was wrong he does not expose the checking device, but merely replaces the card on the table, word uppermost, and the next child takes his turn. The child with the greatest number of cards at the end is the winner. The game can be repeated until no participant makes an error.

Game 2 (b): Pick a word

This game is similar to Game 2 (a) but more difficult, as the cards are placed on the table in a pack, so there is no choice of words to read. Children take it in turn to read aloud the word on the top card. It is then reversed on the table, to reveal the picture. If the child was correct, he keeps the card. If not, the card goes to the bottom of the pack, word uppermost.

Game 3: Can you read my cards?

No. of players: 2
Equipment: 2 different packs of cards (self-checking)

In this game, the children act as testers for each other. Each player has a pack of cards that he can read (previously checked by his teacher). The first child shows the top card in his pile to his opponent. If the second child can read the word, he gains the card and places it on a pile to his right. If not, the first player replaces the card at the bottom of his own pack. Then the second player shows a word to the first player and so on. The winner is the player who first gains all his opponent's cards.

Game 4: Racing

No. of players: 2, 3 or 4
Equipment:
(a) Any pack of self-checking cards
(b) A race-track of any shape marked out on a large piece of card, or blackboard, placed flat on the floor (see fig 3.1).

FIG 3.1 ·   A sample race-track

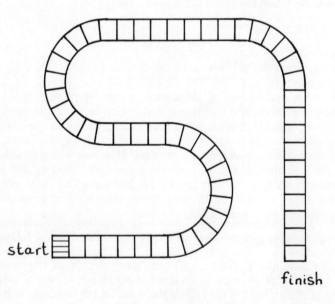

N.B.   The race-track can be of any shape, although one with curves in it usually proves more exciting. The number of spaces round the track will depend upon the number of word cards considered to be appropriate for the game – assuming the length of the 'average' word to be four letters.

(c) 2, 3, or 4 tiny, toy horses, or cars, or counters of different colours. This game can be noisy, as the competitive element is very much enjoyed, so is best played in an area where other children are not working. (In fine weather the race-track can be marked in the playground.) The 'horses' are lined up at the starting tape. The first child tries to read the word or sentence on the top card of the pack and turns the card over for the other jockeys or drivers to check. If he was correct, his 'horse' or 'car' moves along the race-track the relevant number of spaces, i.e. according to the number of letters in the word read, (or words in the sentence). If the player was wrong, his 'horse' does not move. The card goes to the bottom of the pack.

Many of the games already familiar to children, for example, dominoes, snakes and ladders and happy families, can also be used as practice in learning sight words, as follows.

Games 5: Word dominoes

No. of players: 2
Equipment: card dominoes with appropriate words

FIG 3.2   Sample word dominoes

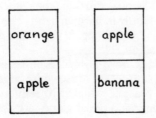

A pack of 28 dominoes will utilise 7 words. In preparing the cards, regard the 7 words as digits and the 28 cards will be represented by the following pairs of words.

1 – 1	2 – 2	3 – 3	4 – 4	5 – 5	6 – 6	7 – 7
1 – 2	2 – 3	3 – 4	4 – 5	5 – 6	6 – 7	
1 – 3	2 – 4	3 – 5	4 – 6	5 – 7		
1 – 4	2 – 5	3 – 6	4 – 7			
1 – 5	2 – 6	3 – 7				
1 – 6	2 – 7					
1 – 7						

The game is then played exactly as with normal dominoes, except that the player must pronounce the word which he is matching to the word on the table.

Game 6: Snakes and Ladders

No. of players: 2 or 3

Equipment: A 'snakes and ladders' board and a small pack of self-checking word cards.

The players take it in turn to read the top card of the pack, and move the appropriate number of squares according to the number of letters in the words that are successfully read. The cards are replaced at the bottom of the pack.

Game 7: Happy families

No. of players: 2 or 3

Equipment: A pack of small word cards belonging to two or three different topics, such as fruit, animals, colours, numbers or vehicles, with checks on the reverse side and an equal number of cards for each topic.

Each 'family' of cards should first be read through by the group, communally, and doubtful words checked by reference to the reverse sides, before all the cards are shuffled together in one pack and placed in the centre of the table with the words uppermost. The players take it in turn to read the top card. If successful, the player takes the card. If not, the card goes to the bottom of the pile. (Players hold their cards carefully to hide the checking devices.) When all the cards from the pack have been captured, the players ask each other for cards in the normal way, in order to complete a family. The player making the request must hold at least one card of that particular family in his own hand. The request should take the form of, 'I'd like to have your "apple" card from the fruit family, please.' Turns move round as before.

Such games represent only a small sample of activities which will motivate children to want to learn to recognise large numbers of words and will afford them the practice which will reinforce their learning in an enjoyable manner. Many additional games are described in the publications listed in Appendix 1.

IV   A system for individual learning and checking of special categories of words

Following a certain amount of practice of sight words in group games, children's speedy recognition of words which they find particularly interesting can be expanded by introducing individual practice relating to special categories of words, such as 'pets', 'birds', 'football' or 'things I like to eat'. The system I have normally used to extend children's mastery of sight words was based mainly on a very large collection of small tin boxes, each containing groups of small cards, the majority of which had self-checking devices on the reverse sides, as described in Chapter 2. I have found this system to work particularly well with children aged from 6 to 9 years and with remedial groups aged from 7 or 8 years up to 13 or 14 years. Once a pupil had reached a Reading Age of about 7–8 years, this system was usually not required, except for words relating to special subjects such as, for example, Mathematics, Science or Cookery, and for characters' names in books currently being read or shown as a series on television. In that event, a chart on the wall, listing names of people and other special words, together with a corresponding box of small cards, provided adequate help for both personal reading and writing activities.

A Individual practice

This system of individual practice and checking of groups of sight words on cards in small boxes, which I consistently employed when teaching children of 6 to 9 years and with remedial groups, turned out to be an activity which the children always enjoyed. The number of cards in each pack was kept sufficiently small for the children to learn all the words in a short space of time, for example, with 6 year olds or very poor readers of any age, 10 or 12 cards were usually sufficient in each box. Older children or better readers could often progress to 20 cards. I suggest that 25 cards in one pack should be regarded as an absolute maximum, as it is preferable for children to learn to recognise two small packs of cards quickly, and have the pleasure of seeing them ticked off, than for them to struggle for too long endeavouring to learn a larger group of words at one time.

This system of individual learning should always be initiated by using a small pack of cards which have self-checking devices on the reverse sides. (The number of cards would depend on the level of reading – up to a maximum of 25.) The child holds the pack of cards, with the words uppermost, in his left hand. It does not matter in which order the words are placed and, indeed, it is a good idea to train him to shuffle the cards before he uses them.

Step 1   The child looks at the top card and says to himself what he thinks the word is. He then reverses that card to check, by means of the illustration on the back, if he were correct. Train him to say to himself: 'If I was *right* (i.e. correct), I put the card on my *right*. If I was *wrong*, I put the card on my *left*.' The child goes through the whole pack in this way, ending with two packs of cards in front of him.

Step 2   For the moment, he ignores the cards on the right, as these represent his successes. He goes through the small pack on his left two or three times, saying each word to himself and then checking on the reverse side to see if he is correct.

Step 3   After two or three correct practice runs with the cards which were in the left-hand pack, these cards are shuffled with those which were on the right. Step 1 is repeated with the complete pack and, if necessary, Steps 2 and 3.

Step 4   When the child has twice or thrice, after reshuffling the whole pack, read all the cards correctly, he is ready to find a 'tester'.

B   Checking by accredited testers

Still working on the principle of saving a teacher's time for the most important tasks in the teaching–learning process, a series of preliminary checks of children's knowledge of word packs, undertaken by people other than the teacher, can be set up.

1   Parents and older siblings

I found that if a child took a box of cards home with him to practice, most parents were very pleased to take the opportunity of spending five or ten minutes with their child, helping him to learn the words, in the manner just suggested. Packs of cards which lacked self-checking devices were ideal for profiting from the assistance of adults and older siblings, in this way, at home.

2   Older pupils in the school

In a similar manner, I found that older pupils in schools, were delighted to help younger children, who were working with boxes of cards which lacked checking devices, by prompting the children when they failed words. Especially on wet or cold lunch-times and break-times, an older pupil would frequently be seen, in a cloakroom or an odd corner, helping a child from a younger class or a remedial group to acquire quick recognition of a pack of sight words. This practice seemed to be enjoyed by both the learner and the helper.

3   Specified pupil testers in the class

The penultimate check, before the learner came to be tested by the teacher, was made by a child-tester in his own class. Nearly every child in the class was a tester at certain levels for, as soon as a child had been checked by the teacher as being absolutely accurate at reading all the words in a particular box of cards, he became an accredited tester himself at that level. This was always an occasion for great pride, and it meant that everyone was continually helping others to improve their performance. I always emphasised to child-testers that they should not pass on to me, for checking, any child who could not immediately read *all* the words in any particular pack. Some budding young teachers were discovered in this process!

V   Methods of recording success

Once a teacher has finally checked that a pupil has instant recognition of a group of words, there are two ways in which these successes can be recorded.

A Teacher's record-book

In order to plan additional practice activities for an individual child or to form a new *ad hoc* group of children who need special practice with a particular group of words, the effective teacher will always need to have accurate records of the words every child does and does not recognise. In Chapter 2, Part IV, an accurate, yet simple, system of record-keeping by the teacher is described, and teachers are recommended to try this system.

B Children's word books

In addition to the teacher's records of the words which individual pupils recognise, it is also helpful for children to keep their own records, in the form of a lexicon or personal dictionary of words which they can read. Many children aged 6 years are able to undertake this task in a simple form and this gives them great satisfaction.

The following suggestions provide a description of individual word books which I have found to be the most successful. At the beginning of a school year or new term, or whenever is judged to be an appropriate moment, provide either every pupil in a class or an appropriate group of children, with a small ruled or squared notebook in which the height of the pages is much greater than the width. On the front cover have a white label which shows the child's name and, underneath it, the title, 'My book of words' or 'I can read these words'. Inside the books, there should be either a single page or, preferably a double spread, for each of the letters of the alphabet. These should be clearly printed at the top of each page or spread, in both upper case and lower case forms. Older pupils can prepare these books for themselves. In the case of younger pupils, older pupils, students or small working parties of parents can help with or undertake this task.

If the teacher wants to introduce a whole class or a group of children to the word books at the same time, she must choose a collection of words which she is certain that they all recognise, for example, the first names of all the pupils in the class, a few very simple words such as 'I', 'a', 'in', 'dog' and 'cat', or a list of colours. A little practice, in unison, either with flash-cards or with the words written on the blackboard, will ensure that everyone in the group or class can actually read the words. As each word is read, the children will be asked to find the appropriate page in their own notebooks and write the word close to the left-hand margin. Later words added on any page will be written in a column underneath the first word. (See Chapter 5 for a suggestion for using the right-hand column of each page for words which are exceptions to general phonic elements or rules.)

Once children have been initiated into the use of these books on a number of occasions by class or group entries, they can be trained to make individual entries. The occasion on which a child has learned to read a particular pack of small cards, and has had it finally checked by his teacher, is a particularly opportune moment for the individual to enter the batch of words, in the appropriate pages in his own notebook.

It is a useful practice, at the end of every week, to have pupils draw a short line under the last word on every page. At the end of every term a double line should be drawn. Teachers are then able to see, at a glance, the quantity of words their pupils have learned to recognise in a week or a term. The children themselves, as well as their parents, find such records gratifying. It was following my discovery that certain children in the 6 to 7-year-old age groups were counting up, at intervals, the total number of words they could read from these notebooks, that I incorporated a place for such totals in their own record-books. A simple table at either the beginning or end of the notebook was devised as in Table 3.1. Such tables can, of course, be made as simple or as complicated as the ages of the pupils warrant. I found that children as young as 7 or 8 years enjoyed having 'cumulative totals'.

TABLE 3.1   Words I can read

Date	Number	Total
Week ending:		
15 September	12	12
22 September	12	24
29 September	20	44
etc		
This term:	259	259

The practice of pupils checking every Friday afternoon the number of words they have each learned to read during the week, also provides an opportunity for revision. Train them to read to themselves each of the words they have mastered during the week. In some cases it might be considered helpful to allow children to take these word books home every week-end so that their parents can check that the children still remember them. I also found it useful revision to allow a few minutes every Monday morning for each child to read to himself the words he had learned to read in the preceding week.

The practice of children recording the number of new words they learn to recognise every week cannot be continued indefinitely. It is only a temporary prop, perhaps for a year or two, or maybe longer with slow-learning children or remedial groups. Only the teacher can judge when it might be helpful to her pupils to commence this practice and when they are ready to discard it because the rate of their mastery of sight vocabulary is continuing to increase so rapidly. For example, if the rate of learning is such that the time taken to acquire rapid recognition of words is shorter than the time it takes the children to record the words, then it is more than probable that the recording activity has outlived its usefulness. (A Reading Age of about 7 years 6 months might prove to be such a stage.) The system can then be superseded by records of 'New words', as described later.

One further point should be noted about children's lists of words they can read: such lists represent a practical and personal basis for learning about the alphabetic order of letters and words – leading to practice in locating words in dictionaries – an important skill of reading, which is considered in Book 3 in this series.

VI Vocabulary extension

For children to become proficient readers, as well as being able to express themselves clearly and appositely in both the spoken and the written word, they need to be encouraged, at every stage, to be interested in words and their meaning. Accordingly, ensuring that pupils of all ages are continually enlarging their vocabulary of words which they can not only pronounce but also understand, should form one of the daily concerns of every teacher. During the first year or two in infant or first schools, this process generally goes on informally, but round about the age of 7 years, this work can benefit from an additional emphasis.

One simple system I developed and used is as follows. In one corner of the blackboard is marked a small oblong, with the heading of 'New words'. During any day, in any class, there are always new and interesting words occurring – in a radio or television programme, in something a visitor says, in a book a child is reading, in a story or in a sentence a pupil has written. Many children enjoy collecting and using new and telling words and those who have not learned the pleasure of this activity need special encouragement. When a new and interesting word occurs on any occasion in a class, the teacher should take a moment or two to draw the attention of the whole class to it and have a brief discussion about it. As an example, take the case of young children's common use of the word 'nice'. Suppose that the word 'delicious' crops up in some context. A few minutes of class discussion will soon reveal that the word usually refers to taste or smell, and children will be quick to provide sentences illustrating examples of nouns to which this adjective can appropriately be attached. In a similar manner, encountering the word 'gigantic' in a story can lead to a discussion of a series of words indicating graded sizes, for example, 'tiny', 'little', 'medium-sized', 'big', 'large', 'huge', 'enormous' and 'gigantic'. The words can be discussed, and young children would enjoy illustrating these words by objects of different sizes. Then the new word or words are written by the teacher in the oblong on the blackboard. The children will not only learn to read them and appreciate their meaning, but they will begin to use them in both their spoken and written language.

A regular routine is established by which, at the end of every afternoon, the word or words are read and their meaning discussed. A similar moment of revision takes place first thing every morning. In most weeks, at least three or four new words have been added to the corner of the blackboard and quite frequently the number is larger than this. At the end of the week, younger children can add these new words to the lists in their personal books entitled 'Words I can read'. It is very important, with younger children, that these 'new words' should only be very small in number, otherwise the exercise will become a chore rather than a pleasurable feeling of achievement. With older pupils and more proficient readers, as mentioned earlier, their personal notebooks can move from 'Words I can read' to 'New words', that is referring more to an enrichment of children's knowledge of the meanings of the words than merely their ability to recognise and pronounce words.

Chapter 4

Mastery of 'Key Words to Literacy'

I 'Key words to Literacy'

A Basic sight words

It was suggested in the preceding chapter that in order to read a book, by himself, in a meaningful manner, the child needs to recognise immediately on sight, at the very least, 95 per cent of the words in the text or more probably 99 per cent of the words. If we add to this the fact that there are 200 words in the English language which make up half to three-quarters of the running words occurring in everyday reading matter – that is adult reading material, not just reading materials for children learning to read – we can begin to realise how vital it is that teachers should ensure that, at the earliest possible stage, children acquire instant recognition of every one of these words. Consequently, although I should certainly not advocate that children's reading tuition should *begin* by mastering these words, it is necessary to emphasise that the words listed in *Key Words to Literacy* (McNally & Murray, 1962) are the most important of all the sight words in a child's reading vocabulary.

B 'Key Words to Literacy'

A number of lists of basic sight words have been published in the USA, for example, the well-known *Basic Sight Vocabulary of 220 Words* (Dolch, 1945). It was not until 1962, however, that McNally & Murray's list of 200 basic sight words, *Key Words to Literacy* was published in England. Even so, despite the importance and usefulness of these 200 words, in both reading and writing, there are still very many teachers who are unaware of the vital role they play in all literacy training.

The authors of *Key Words to Literacy* stated that the following 12 words form over a quarter of all the running words in both juvenile and adult reading materials:

a	and	he	I	in	is
it	of	that	the	to	was

When the following 20 words are added, the total of 32 words represents approximately 39 per cent of all juvenile and adult reading materials:

all	as	at	be	but	are	for	had	have	him
his	not	on	one	said	so	they	we	with	you

The first 100 words account for 56·9 per cent of juvenile and 51·8 per cent of adult reading matter. When a further 100 words are added, the total of 200 words represents over two-thirds of juvenile reading material and slightly less than two-thirds of adult reading matter. These figures very clearly indicate the significance of these words for fluent reading at every level.

McNally & Murray had the following to say about when 'key words' should be known and whether they considered the situation in this respect to be satisfactory in 1962:

'They are key words in verbal communication for child and adult. Their immediate recognition is essential for fluent reading. No matter the age at which the average child enters a formal reading programme the aim should be to have him read these words with little or no hesitation some time towards the end of his second year of reading. At present, many children with reading ages around 6½ do not know enough of these words, children reading about the 7 to 7½ years old level do not quite know them all; or, if they do, their recognition is slow and hesitant in too many cases. With older backward children the aim should be to make the words known as soon as possible.'

C   How well known are 'key words'?

More recently, the Schools Council project: *Extending Beginning Reading* (Southgate *et al.*, 1981) provided data, based on information obtained in 1974, concerning the mastery of the first 200 'key words' by pupils aged 8 years and 9 years. The 197 pupils concerned came from 57 primary schools in the north-west of England. The younger age-group was made up of 121 children, each of whose Chronological Age, and Reading Age on Schonell's *Graded Word Reading Test* (Schonell, 1948), was 8 years 0 months (plus or minus 2 months). The older group consisted of 76 children whose Chronological Ages and Reading Ages were, correspondingly 9 years 0 months (plus or minus 2 months). The children were tested individually by being asked to read aloud the first 200 'key words' from typewritten sheets; the number of errors being recorded in each case. The results were as shown in Table 4.1.

TABLE 4.1 Percentages of pupils of average reading ability making errors in reading the first 200 words of *Key Words to Literacy*

| No. of | Percentage of pupils | |
errors	Aged 8	Aged 9
0	20	31
1–3	29	49
4–6	19	11
7–9	15	5
10 and over	17	4

The picture presented is that 20 per cent of average readers of 8 years and 31 per cent of average readers of 9 years could read all 200 words immediately on sight. At the other end of the scale, in the category of 10 or more errors, the range of errors for 8 year old was 10–35, and for 9 year olds it was 10–12. Although the results for 9 year olds do show an improvement on the figures for 8 year olds, I do not think that they can be taken as indicating that teachers had developed a general policy of, first, diagnosing the errors made by younger children in their recognition of 'key words' and then setting in motion plans to rectify deficiencies. Indeed, the indications are that the reverse is true. To pin-point the actual words which children do not recognise and to promote activities which will ensure absolute success is a simple matter, as will be shown later in this chapter. Had such teaching–learning strategies been put into effect with 6 year olds and 7 year olds, in the schools in question, these average readers aged 8 and 9 years would have recognised *instantly* all 200 'key words'. Moreover, as these 200 words represent more than two-thirds of the running total of words in juvenile reading materials, these 'average' readers would, no doubt, have been able to read at a considerably higher level.

The most disturbing implication of Table 4.1, however, arises from the fact that it refers to children of average reading ability and not to children of below average reading ability. This fact causes one to wonder how many of these 200 'key words', 8 and 9-year-old children of below average reading ability fail to recognise, and also how many 'failing readers' could soon be helped to become competent readers if their failures in this area were diagnosed and appropriate teaching–learning activities introduced.

II Timing the learning of 'key words'

While I agree entirely with McNally & Murray's earlier statement that many children with Reading Ages of about 6½ do not know sufficient of these 'key words', I should like to add a small note of caution. Nothing would be more likely to cause young children or failing older readers to dislike reading than to launch into a heavy teaching programme of discrete words which have neither interest nor meaning for them. The problem is that the majority of the most commonly used words in our language are neither nouns nor adjectives. For example, the first 32 of the most frequently used words (set our earlier) are words which are not easy for young children to learn because they do not carry with them, in isolation, either the meaning or the interest of words like 'Mummy', 'Daddy', 'dog' or 'ice-cream', which most young children learn to read fairly early and quite easily. Nevertheless, the introduction of interesting activities can ensure that even these dull words can be learned quite happily – as is suggested later in this chapter.

To be specific about when and when not to begin teaching 'key words': these words should certainly not be any child's introduction to learning to read. In the 5 to 6-year-old age-group, towards the end of a child's first year of schooling would be an appropriate time for the teacher to begin to check his recognition of the first and most important group of 12 'key words', provided that by then he already recognises many interesting words and has enjoyed the experience of reading some simple books. Some children, towards the end of their first year in school, will be ready for this, while other children will not. Only the teacher can decide.

If I were a teacher of a class of children aged 6–7 years or 7–8 years, the first thing I should do at the beginning of a school year would be to help all my pupils to find books which they were capable of reading on their own. Secondly, I should take the poorest readers, as long as they had some ability to read simple sentences and continuous prose, and check their knowledge of the first 12 'key words'. With pupils in older classes and with remedial classes and groups, the same procedure would be adopted, except for those children who were clearly fluent readers, having Reading Ages of perhaps 9 or 10 years.

III   Teaching, practising, checking and recording

Teaching and/or arranging for appropriate practice whereby learning will take place, checking or testing whether the learning has been accomplished, and arranging for further practice activities if the learning has not taken place, form a continous process of good tuition. On different occasions the teacher will choose to intervene at different points in this continuing circle. If we think first of the teacher facing a new class of pupils of any age-group from 6 year olds to 9 year olds, I should advise breaking into this circle by checking or testing.

A Checking, testing and recording

1 Checking by using cards

The two most accurate ways in which a teacher can discover the extent of her pupils' mastery of 'key words' each require individual administration. To discover the exact 'key words' which a young or less proficient reader recognises and those he fails to recognise, small packs of 'key words' cards are required. These cards can be hand-made, as suggested Chapter 3, or they can be purchased from Ladybirds Books Limited (see Appendix 2). The first 200 cards should be divided into small packs, as follows, and then each pack placed in a small tin or cardboard box and labelled.

Pack 1: The 12 most important words;
Pack 2: The 20 next most important words;
Packs 3(a), (b) and (c): The next 68 words, divided into 3 packs;
Packs 4(a), (b), (c) and (d): The second 100 words, divided into 4 packs;
Packs 5(a) and (b): The additional 50 nouns, divided into 2 packs.

(See Appendix 3 for the actual words which might be included in each pack.)

Having first helped all the children in the class to select books they can read easily and provided them with opportunities to read these books to themselves, the teacher should then spend a minute or two with one pupil who is clearly one of the least efficient readers in the class. She should place in this child's hands the pack of 12 cards which form Pack 1, stacked in the order suggested, and ask him to read the word on the top card. When he reads it, or fails to read it, she asks him to place the card at the bottom of the pack and try the next word. This is continued until the child has gone right through the pack.

While the child is doing this, the teacher is recording his failures on a duplicated sheet of lists of 'key words' which she has in front of her. Appendix 3 provides an example of appropriate individual record sheets. The words within each pack of cards are arranged in what I consider to be the easiest order for children to learn. If this order is adopted, the appropriate pack number and card number should be marked on the back of each card. When the child reads a word correctly no mark is required on the record sheets. Every word which the child fails to read correctly should be circled. (On a retest, ticks can be put against correct responses to words which were incorrect at the original testing.) When the child has gone right through one small pack, the total number of words he read correctly can be entered into the teacher's record-book, as described in Chapter 2, section IV. If the child read all the words in Pack 1 correctly, he can try the next pack, unless the checking session is becoming unduly long. As soon as the child reaches a pack of these cards in which he does not know all the words, the teacher has found a point of reference for prescribing teaching–learning activities for that particular child.

2   Checking by using test sheets

Those children, whom the teacher's observations have led her to conclude know some of the 'key words' but not all of them, can be tested individually by the teacher providing a child with a duplicated sheet of key words, set out in columns and sub-divided into manageable groups. (The lists of words shown in Appendix 3 would provide suitable test sheets.) The teacher needs an identical test sheet in front of her, for use as a record form. It is worth noting, at this point, that discrete words should always be presented to children in vertical columns rather than in horizontal lines, as the latter should always be regarded by children as phrases, sentences and paragraphs which have meaning for them. The child is asked to read down the columns of test words until he is told to stop. He should be stopped whenever he reaches a group of words in which he makes more than one or two errors. As before, the teacher is circling words failed on her own sheet and later she will complete her own record-book by ticking categories completely correct and pencilling in the number of correct responses in categories where there were some errors.

If the child makes only a very few errors on the whole sheet, the teacher can print these particular words on a card for him or he can do this himself. Later he can practise reading these few words and return, on another day, to have them checked. If the child's level of competence is found to extend only part of the way through the lists, the teacher is then in a position to prescribe for him learning activities on a particular group of words. Such activities will probably take the form of participating in a group game, followed by individual practice with a box of cards, as described in Chapter 3.

Although I have suggested using test sheets of 'key words', for testing children's knowledge individually, McNally & Murray, in their booklet *Key Words to Literacy* (1971), do provide a suggestion of a group test which can be carried out by having each child provided with a duplicated sheet of the first 200 'key words', presented in a particular format. The teacher has a simple set of words printed on thin card. As she reads words from her card, the pupils are asked to find each word on their own sheets and to make a particular mark on it, for example a ring round it or a cross on top of it. The same test card or sheet can also be used for individual tests to assess children's speed of recognition and also to contrast their ability to read phonically based words as opposed to irregular words. (These test cards and duplicated sheets can be purchased from the Schoolmaster Publishing Company – see Appendix 2.)

B   Teaching and learning activities

As it is highly unlikely that there will ever be a whole class ready to learn certain 'key words' at the same time or, alternatively, that the mastery of these words by the pupils in any one class will be so diverse that individual tuition is essential, let us assume that most of the teaching and the practice necessary for effective learning will take the form of group activities. It could be a group of children whom the teacher has deemed ready to learn the first 12 'key words'. Alternatively, it could be a group of children who can recognise the first 100 words and are ready for learning some of the second 100 words.

Many of the teaching and learning activities described in Chapter 3 are equally relevant to the learning of 'Key Words to Literacy'. The teacher can still use large flash-cards to provide small groups of children with practice in recognising single words. Many of the group games described, as well as the individual learning and checking activities and the teacher's method of recording, all have relevance for 'key words'. There are, however, two main problems which 'key words' pose in contrast to 'interesting' sight words. First, they are nearly all dull words for children to learn, as opposed to the many nouns in the categories of 'interesting' words and, secondly, the majority of 'key words' do not lend themselves to having checking devices on the reverse sides of small cards.

The result of the lack of self-checking devices for these words is that, while groups of children can still play many of the group games suggested in Chapter 3 and in the publications listed in Appendix 1, the group games will need to be in the charge of a teacher, student or other adult, or a child in the class who is a better reader, knowing the particular group of words being practised, so that he can act as a referee.

There is, however, one other method which I have employed and which sometimes overcomes the problem of needing a referee when cards lack checking devices: its effectiveness depends largely on the ages and competencies of the children concerned. In practice, when three or four children are assigned to a game, using a particular pack of 'key words', their teacher has carefully selected them as an *ad hoc* group on the criterion that none of them has immediate recognition of *all* the words in that pack. It follows that, for each word in the pack, there may well be someone in the group who can read it and so can confirm or refute another child's reading of that word. Consequently, one child player is given the additional role of referee for that day. This means that if there is any disagreement as to the correctness of a player's response, the child-referee takes the card to the teacher or to a designated 'child-tester' who will tell him what the word is.

It is because 'key words' are intrinsically so uninteresting that it is a good plan to reserve the most exciting games for providing practice in recognising these words. The following are a few of the games which I have found to be most popular with children in different age groups and which, consequently, I usually reserve for practising 'key words'.

Game 8: Fishing

No. of players: 2 or 3

Equipment: A deep cardboard box to represent a fish tank; 12–20 cardboard 'fish' with paperclips in their mouths; a magnet attached to a piece of string and a rod, as a fishing line.

'Fishing' is a game which young children of about the age of 6 years enjoy. The first 12 'key words' or, if these are known, the next 20 words are each printed on a separate cardboard fish. The fish are placed in the bottom of the box, which can be painted blue or covered with blue paper to represent water. The children take it in turn to try to 'fish' in the tank. When a child catches a fish, he can keep it, as long as he can read the word. If he cannot read it correctly, the fish must be thrown back in the tank. When the tank is empty, the winner is the child with the most fish. A child adjudicator is required for this game, that is someone who has previously had his own recognition of all the words being used checked by the teacher.

One of the games which I have found to be most popular with all ages of children from 7 years upwards, including remedial readers in secondary schools, and which, consequently, I usually reserve for practising 'key words' is 'bingo', played as follows.

Game 9: Bingo

No. of players: 4

Equipment: 4 boards of coloured card relating to the group of words to be practised; a pack of cards as described below

This game is, of course, very similar to the game played by adults. Special boards have to be made for each pack of cards which requires practising. The boards should be made of coloured card, in order that the small white cards, when placed on the board, will show up against the coloured background and so highlight the words not yet covered. Each of the four boards needs to be ruled into 9 oblongs – 3 rows of 3 – and each oblong needs to be slightly larger than the size of the small cards which will form the pack. Words relating to a particular pack of cards are printed, one on each oblong, on the four boards. Care needs to be taken in the arrangement of words to be printed in the spaces, as no two boards should have the same selection of words and, preferably, the same word should not appear twice on any board. For example if a set of boards is designed for practising the second 20 'key words', two identical packs of cards of these words will be required. The first 20 cards can be allocated according to the numbers on the boards in Fig. 4.2. As only 16 cards from the second pack will be required to complete the boards, discard the easiest four words. (For examples, 'at', 'as', 'on' and 'not'.) The remaining 16 cards can be placed on the remaining spaces, one per card, in rotation, avoiding repetition.

Once the person preparing the boards has all the spaces on the four boards covered with small white cards and is satisfied with their arrange-

FIG. 4.1 Fishing

FIG. 4.2 Examples of four bingo boards for 'key words' Pack 2

Board
1

but [1]	for	we
be [13]	not [5]	said
one	are [17]	him [9]

Board
2

said [10]	we [2]	have
they	one [14]	had [6]
but	him	for [18]

Board
3

all [19]	at [11]	so [3]
you	had	they [15]
on [7]	with	his

Board
4

are	have [20]	his [12]
as [4]	so	be
you [16]	with [8]	all

N.B.   The small numbers indicate the order in which the first 20 small cards are laid out on the boards.

ment, one small card at a time can be removed and the word on it printed clearly on the space on the board. Each board will then require a reference number on the reverse side and possibly also a title. The appropriate number of small cards for playing the game can then be kept together in a small box or plastic bag, appropriately labelled. Teachers who do not have helpers, such as parents' groups, who are willing to undertake some of the work of preparing such apparatus, may prefer to purchase sets of equipment for this game from Galt & Co. (see Appendix 2), under the title of *Key Words Lotto Games*.

Bingo is best played, in the first instance, with the teacher in charge. Each child sits with a board in front of him. The teacher exposes one card to the child on her left. If he has this word on his board *and can read the word* on the teacher's small card, he receives the card and covers the word on his board. If not, the teacher places the card at the bottom of the pack and shows the next card to the next child. This process continues until one child has his board completely full, and he is declared the winner. The pack is then shuffled and the game starts again with a different child having the first turn. When all the children are familiar with the game and fairly confident about the words in a particular pack of cards, a 'child-tester' may act as the referee and be in charge of the cards. Playing this game will eventually be followed by individual children practising with the 12 card pack from a tin box, as described earlier, and finally each child's recognition of the words will be checked and recorded by his teacher. This successful child will then become a member of a group who are playing a game relating to the next pack of 'key words' cards.

Game 4: Racing, which was described in Chapter 3 can be used for practising 'key words' provided that a 'child-adjudicator', who can read all the words, is used. In the same way, many other words which are not suitable for self-checking devices, can be used satisfactorily to play some of the games described in Chapter 3. A word of warning is probably in order at this point. A child referee or adjudicator should only ever spend a very small proportion of his time in helping other children who are less proficient than himself. As there will usually be many children in a class who are completely familiar with the 'key words' which poorer readers are practising, it should be simple to use the competent readers, in this way, on a rota system.

Two games of *Memory* are also quite useful for practising 'key words' either with the teacher present to supervise or with a child-adjudicator.

Game 10: Memory (a)

No. of players: 3 or 4
Equipment: 1 pack of small words cards
The cards are spread out randomly, i.e. not in aligned rows, face-downwards on a small table. The children take it in turn to choose a card and turn it over so that all the others can see it. If the child can read it

correctly he retains it: if not, he turns if face-downwards on the table, *in the exact position* in which he found it. The remaining children take it in turn to reverse one card and try to read it. When all the cards have been removed from the table, the winner is the one with the most cards. The cards can then be reshuffled and spread out again on the table, face downwards, for a second game. The next child will have first turn.

Game 11: Memory (b)

No. of players: 3 or 4
Equipment: 2 packs of identical small cards
The game is played similarly to 'Memory (a)'. The two packs of cards are shuffled together and spread out face downwards on the table. The children take it in turn to reverse any two cards on the table so that everyone can see them. If the words are the same, the child tries to pronounce them and, if he is successful, keeps them. If not, the cards are turned back in the same positions. (It will be found that these two 'memory' games are usually played very quietly because children are concentrating on remembering where certain word cards are lying on the table.)

C   Returning to checking and recording

Playing in group games with 'key words' cards will, at a certain stage, need to be followed by individual children practising reading the words from the small packs of cards on their own. But as the cards have no self-checking devices on the reverse sides, the child will need to have someone who can read all the words in the pack. 'Key words' cards are the ideal packs of cards for children to take home and practise, with their parents acting as checkers. The children can then bring the packs of cards back to school, find an appropriate child-tester', and finally be checked by the teacher and have the results recorded on their 'key words' record sheet and in the teacher's record-book. Thus the circle is completed and a new set of words for learning can be introduced.

IV   How important are discrete words?

Two of the chapters in this book, that is Chapters 3 and 4, have been devoted mainly to learning activities related to recognition of discrete words; many of the activities taking the form of group games which children will enjoy playing. The more fluent children become in reading, the less they will need to practise recognition of sight words until, finally, a stage will be reached when this side of reading tuition is completely phased out. It would be unfortunate, however, if teachers were to take this emphasis on quick recognition of discrete words to imply that the major portion of children's time in reading periods should be spent in this way. On the contrary, such activities should only form the minor part of a varied reading programme. The major proportion of children's time – and this proportion will grow larger as the children become older and as their proficiency in reading increases – should be devoted to individual, silent reading of continuous prose, in the form of books which they themselves have selected and which their teachers know that they *can* read.

PART THREE

Techniques for Tackling Unfamiliar Words

Chapter 5

Utilising contextual clues

I Understanding

Understanding is the prime characteristic of reading; indeed there is little point in either a child or an adult being able to pronounce or 'read' separate words unless the global act of reading makes sense to him. To achieve this, the reader's eyes need to be constantly moving along the lines of print, grouping words into meaningful phrases, sentences and larger units, such as paragraphs and chapters. His inward eye, that is his mind, needs to be absorbing the message underlying the printed words almost as if a film were unrolling before his eyes. This applies whether the words constitute a notice, a poster, a story, information or instructions for using a new piece of equipment.

Consequently in Book 1 in this series, *Children who do read*, the whole concern was with arranging for children, at as early an age as possible, to spend ever-increasing periods of time on personal reading. However, as indicated earlier in this book, for a child's eyes to travel swiftly and smoothly along the lines of print, processing the words into meaningful messages, he must be able to recognise instantly about 99 per cent of the words he encounters. If this is not so, the child's hesitations and halts will impede, or entirely destroy, the flow of meaning which the words and sentences would have conveyed to him, had he been able to move ahead rapidly without these pauses.

The preceding chapters have concentrated on ways of helping pupils to increase their sight vocabulary, by participating, for a small proportion of their 'reading time', in group or individual activities designed to enlarge the store of words which they can recognise immediately on sight. At the same time, it should not be forgotten that, in the act of continous reading itself, the reader is inevitably learning to recognise and understand new words. This is just as true for the child who is able to read simple continuous prose as it is for the effective adult reader. Smith (*Reading*, 1978) provides us with a telling example of how, in his words:

' . . . through reading we can add enormously to our understanding of all the words in our language. Put in everyday terms, we learn the meanings of words . . . in written language the clues to meaning usually come from the context. You may not know what the word *rundlet* means, but if you read that a seaman was carrying a rundlet of rum on his shoulders from the stores to his ship, you would probably guess that it was something like a small barrel – and you would be right.'

Let me give a personal, and somewhat more difficult example, of how an adult may learn the meaning of a word not previously encountered by using the clues provided by the context. I began to read a paper by Goodman *et al.* (1978). I was particularly interested in what the authors had to say, and I did not want to be held up in the process of getting their message. Near the beginning of the paper, I came across the following sentence: 'We will present a brief overview of the ontogeny of reading.' I did not recall ever having come across the word 'ontogeny' before, but I was too eager to read the whole article to want to stop, at that stage, to look up its meaning in a dictionary. I continued to read – and understand – the pages that followed. Later in the paper I came to a heading which read, 'Ontogeny of reading'. I read on, and then there appeared the sentence: 'We decided to find out more about the onset of learning to read'; and a little later, 'In order to understand the beginnings of oral language de-velopment . . .' Finally, the following sentence occurred:

'Since our view of reading suggests that a reader is an active participant in learning to read, we began to wonder about the emergence of reading.'

I then had available three separate clues to the meaning of 'ontogeny': they were the words 'onset', 'beginnings' and 'emergence'. Even had I been on holiday when I read the article, without dictionaries available to me, I should have still been able to 'guess' correctly, from these clues in the text, the meaning of the word that I did not, at first, recognise or understand.

When I had finished reading the paper and grasped its message, I took the step of corroborating my conception of the meaning of the word 'ontogeny' by consulting two dictionaries. The *Concise Oxford Dictionary* (Fowler & Fowler, 1964) supplied me with the word 'genesis', while *A Dictionary of Reading and Related Terms* (Harris & Hodges, 1981), pro-vided two definitions, as follows:

1 The origin and development of an individual;
2 The development of a specific behaviour pattern in a lifetime, as *the ontogeny of a person's speech habits.*

These dictionary definitions merely confirmed what I had 'guessed' that the word 'ontogeny' might mean, as my reading of the paper had con-tinued and each of the three clues, in the shape of nouns, had reinforced my awareness of the meaning of this word.

The foregoing description of an adult first passing over an unfamiliar word, then later being helped by clues in the text to formulate an approx-

imation to its meaning and, finally, corroborating the 'guess' by reference
to a dictionary, is a pattern of learning teachers and other educators will be
familiar with through their own reading. Consequently, they will appreciate that it is a method of vocabulary extension which will be helpful to
their pupils. I am aware that certain teachers might be hesitant about
allowing, or encouraging, children to omit words in their silent reading.
Yet, if teachers truly regard reading as understanding the message in the
text, they will also be aware that it is only fluent reading which will draw
forth the meaning. Every hesitation, every pause, every halt, detracts from
the swift movement of eyes along the lines of print and, therefore, lessens
the possibility of comprehension. We, as adults, read books in which we
are interested and we enjoy them, even if we do skip over the odd word. So
do children. Furthermore, I am certain that they should not be chided for
this practice.

Indeed, if a teacher is listening to an individual child, reading aloud, to
her, provided his reading ability has developed beyond the beginning
stage, and the child is unable to read a particular word, the teacher would
be helping him to develop good reading strategies if she suggested that he
read ahead to the end of the sentence and then tried to 'guess' what the
word might be.

In the Schools Council research project, *Extending Beginning Reading*
(Southgate *et al.*, 1981), the strategies which children aged 7 to 9+ used,
when they encountered words which they did not recognise as they were
reading silently to themselves, were investigated in individual interviews
by asking: 'If you come to a word you don't know, when you are reading
by yourself, what do you do about it?' Many of the children mentioned
more than one tactic. The two tactics which headed the list were : asking
someone for help – usually the teacher; and using phonic skills – that is,
either 'sounding out' the word or breaking it up into groups of letters. The
next two responses, in order, were 'guesses the word' and 'misses it out'.
There were only two responses, and these were in the 8 to 9-year-old
age-group, which referred to consulting a dictionary. Although we cannot
be sure that these are the tactics which children actually used, it seems
fairly certain that the first two are the tactics which they had been trained
to use, that is asking the teacher or 'sounding it out'. With the children
who admitted to 'guessing' or missing out the word, these tactics were
never suggested as a first line of attack and quite often the children only
admitted to such tactics when they were pressed. Other children stated
quite firmly that they *never* missed out a word.

Consider how the two main tactics mentioned affect the flow of
children's silent reading and, consequently, impede the process of comprehension. The first tactic, that is asking the teacher, is the worst
offender in this respect, especially if it involves the child joining a queue of
other children who are waiting at the teacher's table, as being the only
means of gaining her attention. By the time the child has chatted to other
children in the queue and wandered back to his seat (probably with little

sorties on the way, to talk with friends), he will almost certainly have lost the flow of the story line. The second tactic, the use of phonic clues, may be helpful if the word is phonically regular, but even so, having to stop in order to try to puzzle out the word will interrupt the process of gaining meaning from the text. The chances are, however, that the word may not be phonically regular, as many of the most commonly used words in our language are irregular. In that event, the child's effort to read the unknown word may prove unsuccessful and he may *then* have to take up even more time in going out to ask his teacher.

II   Aids to comprehension

A   The reader's need to comprehend

There is, within both children and adults, a drive to understand the objects with which they are surrounded. They *want* to know what is going on in the world around them: they have the need to understand what they see and hear and read. The things around them do not merely appear to them as isolated objects: on the contrary, they form an understandable pattern. Even a very young child does not regard the mug on the table as merely a discrete, unmovable object. He knows that it may contain tea or coffee or milk or fruit juice, and that he or his parents may pick up the object and drink from it if they are thirsty. In the same way, children *want* to understand – to make sense of – the words on the pages in their books. They are not likely to do this if they continue to treat each word as an isolated object, without trying to connect it, from the beginning, with the surrounding words and phrases.

The frustrations which children feel when they cannot make sense of what they are trying to read is obvious in the following two quotations from *Extending Beginning Reading* (op. cit.). The children concerned were reporting on books they had tried to read but had *not* enjoyed.

As one boy commented, 'When I was reading it I could not understand what was going on.' This comment is hardly surprising in the light of the fact that the boy who had tried to read this particular book was a 7-year-old of average reading ability and the book in question was *Heroes and Saints*. An 8-year-old boy of above average reading ability was equally frustrated when he had tried to read *Sir and Abu Kir*, a book which was clearly too difficult for him. He wrote:

> '. . . it did not make much sense to me . . . I could not work this book out. I do not know what the author of that book was trying to tell the owner of it. I thought he had not concentrated enough to make a good story.'

This need to make sense of what they are reading gives an impetus to children's reading, provided that the books they have chosen, or have been given, are within their capabilities.

The drive within the reader to make sense of the text he is attempting to read leads him, when he encounters an unknown word, to *predict* what it is likely to be. The word he tries out, when he approaches the word causing him difficulty, may be termed by teachers as a 'guess', and when they describe it in this way, they are really thinking of a 'blind guess'. Yet it is rarely so. The word the child tries out is much more likely to be a prediction of the likelihood of the meaning of the word, based on his understanding of what the preceding text has conveyed to him and his global knowledge of the subject matter about which he is reading. As he reads on, he will begin to appreciate whether or not his prediction was correct – just as I did in the example, described earlier, of the word 'ontogeny'.

Smith (1979), in his book *Reading without Nonsense*, has this to say about prediction:

'To summarize: the basis of comprehension is prediction and prediction is achieved by making use of what we already know about the world, by making use of the theory of the world in the head. There is no need to teach children to predict, it is a natural process, they have been doing it since they were born. Prediction is a natural part of living: without it we would have been overcome by the world's uncertainty and ambiguity long before we arrived at school.'

We have here, then, two aids to comprehension within the reader himself; his need to make sense of what he is reading and his propensity to predict what the unknown word might be likely to be. Hence my suggestion in Chapter 1 that, when a child is reading aloud to a teacher and he meets an unrecognisable word, the teacher's most helpful preliminary response would be to ask the child, 'What do you think it might be?'

B Clues within the text

A further aid to the child, in comprehending what he is trying to read, is inherent in the text itself, which inevitably contains clues which he can use to help him. Psycholinguists such as, for example, Kenneth Goodman, tend to use the word 'cues', instead of clues. The three types of cues usually differentiated are termed 'sematic', 'syntactic' and 'phonic' cues. The first relates to the meanings of words, the second relates to the grammatical arrangements of words in a language, while the third is concerned with sound–symbol relationships. (See also the Glossary in Appendix 5.) *A Dictionary of Reading and Related Terms* (Harris & Hodges 1981) provides the following definitions for these terms.

'*semantic cue* – evidence from the general sense or meaning of a written or spoken communication that aids in the identification of an unknown word.'

'syntactic cue – evidence from a knowledge of the rules and patterns of language that aids in the identification of an unknown word from the way in which it is used.'

'phonic cue – evidence in a spelling pattern in a word of the speech sound or sounds represented by a letter or group of letters.'

The following example indicates how a child may be using or failing to use certain of these cues. Consider the situation in which a child is reading aloud to his teacher and he comes to the sentence, 'Mr and Mrs Smith's home in London was very small.' A child who read the word 'house' instead of 'home', would be using correctly the semantic cues of the remaining words in the sentence, for the word 'house' makes sense in the context of the sentence. The word is also grammatically correct, and so the child could also be said to have used a syntactic cue – an appropriate noun, in this case. He may even have partially used phonic cues in the form of the initial 'h' in the word 'home', and possibly even 'ho', as well as the final 'e'. The teacher has learned that, although the child's knowledge of phonics may be sketchy, nevertheless he is using semantic and syntactic cues correctly, in other words he appreciates that the text should make sense.

If the child in question had been reading aloud to the teacher and, rather than guess the word 'home', had hesitated, the teacher could have helped him by asking 'What do you think the word might be?' If he said 'house' instead of 'home', her response might be, 'Yes, house would make sense here but, if you look more closely you will see that the word doesn't say "house", although it looks something like it.' At this stage, the teacher may wish to probe his knoweldge of phonics by saying 'You were right about the first sound in the word, it does say *h*, but what comes next?' If the child says *o*, the teacher will remind him of the rule of the silent 'e' making the preceding vowel say its name. She will also make a note to ensure that he has further practice in this rule. (See, for example, *Sounds and Words* Book 2 (Southgate & Havenhard, 1961), as well as the games and other activities suggested in Chapter 6 in this book.) If the teacher adopts this sort of attitude, she is placing phonic cues in what I would consider to be their most approriate place, that is the third tactic to use. (Suggestions of ways in which teachers might help children to learn about phonics are put forward in Chapter 6.)

III   Teachers' awareness of the importance of contextual cues

A   Teachers' beliefs

The conclusions I have drawn, from a wide experience of teaching pupils of all ages from 5 to 14 years, of being engaged in remedial education, and of visiting schools in many parts of the country, is that one of the problems about training children to use contextual cues is that the majority of teachers of reading have been conditioned to believe that the most appropriate tactic for helping children to progress from the beginning stages of reading to the fluency represented by a Reading Age of, say, about 9 years 6 months, is to tell the child what the word is which is puzzling him or to ask him to 'sound it out'. Whereas to suggest that the child 'guesses', that is predicts what the unknown word might be, within the context of the sentence or paragraph, and then confirms its accuracy by considering whether or not the word he had predicted makes sense in the context and, if necessary, utilising phonic cues at that point, would be likely to prove a more effective means of promoting children's understanding of what they are reading. For example, supposing a child is reading orally to his teacher and he comes to the sentence:

'They were all having toast and marmalade for breakfast.'

The child does not recognise the word 'toast' but, as his eyes skim along the remainder of the words in the sentence, he recalls that at home his family eats marmalade on bread at breakfast time. Consequently, he 'reads' the word 'bread' instead of 'toast'. This makes sense in the sentence. The word is semantically acceptable. In this case, the teacher could say, 'Yes, "bread and marmalade" makes sense, but look at that word again. Does it start with "b"?' The child will look at the word again and, using phonic cues alongside his search for a word which will make sense in the context, is likely to respond with the word 'toast'.

Smith (op. cit.) points out the usefulness of a knowledge of phonics, for the same purpose as I have just outlined, that is for confirming one's original predictions. He states:

> 'Phonics will in fact prove of use – provided you have a rough idea of what a word is in the first place. If you know that the word you are looking at is probably *horse, cow* or *donkey*, phonics will enable you to tell the difference. But here you do not have to run through all eleven* alternatives for the first two letters of *horse* – you just have to know that a word beginning with *ho* could not be "cow" or "donkey". And you certainly do not have to work your way through the entire word, "blending" all the possible combinations of sounds.'

(I would agree with the sense of this except for the last sentence, on the grounds that a child who does not recognise the word 'horse' will certainly not be aware that it may be possible to pronounce 'ho' at the beginning of a word in eleven different ways. Neither would most adults be aware of this!)

---

* Smith had indicated earlier in the text that the eleven alternative pronunciations of *ho* to which he is referring occur in the following eleven common words – 'hot', 'hope', 'hook', 'hoot', 'house', 'hoist', 'horse', 'horizon', 'honey', 'how', 'honest'.

B   Teachers' knowledge

Some teachers of reading in the United Kingdom seem reluctant to train children to use the context to bring meaning to those words or phrases which they do not instantly recognise. They would feel rather guilty if children were 'guessing' words which they did not know. Such a practice would seem to them to be a reflection on the thoroughness of their own teaching. If I am right about this, why are many teachers reluctant to encourage children to use contextual cues? I think that the answer can be found in the fact that not all teachers are knowledgeable about the value of contextual cues in helping children's understanding of the material they are trying to read.

If teachers are not as knowledgeable about this aspect of learning to read as they might wish, how has this come about? Teachers who completed their initial teacher training before about 1972 would not, of course, have studied this aspect of reading, as the majority of their tutors at that time were unlikely to have been knowledgeable about it. This means that the majority of teachers currently in our schools were not trained to encourage children to use contextual cues. On the other hand, certain teachers have, since their initial training, attended courses of in-service education relating to reading or gone on to take higher qualifications in reading, either at the Open University or in the form of advanced diplomas at other Universities and Colleges of Higher Education. The use of contextual cues would almost certainly have formed part of the curriculum of such courses. Even so, there is still a sizeable proportion of teachers who have not received specific training about the use of contextual cues in reading.

Probably another reason why some teachers have been slow to accept a view of reading which emphasises the importance of contextual cues is that most of the early publications emphasising the importance of meaning in learning to read, rather than the idea of 'cracking the code', were published abroad rather than in the United Kingdom. Frank Smith in Canada and Kenneth Goodman in the USA were two of the writers who expressed such views early in the 1970s. Frank Smith's book *Understanding Reading* (1971) had, as its sub-title 'A Psycholinguistic Analysis of Reading and Learning to Read'. This book was followed, among other publications, by two books entitled *Psycholinguistics and Reading* (Smith, 1973) and *Reading without Nonsense* (Smith, 1979) – originally published in England under the title of *Reading* (Smith, 1978). In the early 1970s not nearly as many professional books on reading, which had been published abroad, found their way into the United Kingdom as do nowadays. Consequently, as far as the majority of practising teachers have been concerned, the fact that many of the earlier publications in this area were published abroad and that the authors were usually classed as 'psycholinguists' – a title unlikely to appeal to practising teachers – was probably sufficient to make them reject the ideas without closely examining them.

Yet the idea of using the context to provide clues to meaning (and without necessarily using the term 'psycholinguistics') has been expounded in various publications in this country for many years. For example, John Merritt presented a paper, entitled 'The Intermediate Skills', to the the Annual Conference of the United Kingdom Reading Association in 1969, in which he said:

'. . . recognition of each successive word is speeded up when context cues are used effectively in fluent reading.'

He went on to say,

'This immediately moves the emphasis in teaching reading to the development of all those skills which lead to accurate anticipation'

(Merritt, 1970).

Other publications in the United Kingdom have followed this theme, for example, *A Language for Life* (Bullock Report, D.E.S., 1975) states:

'The most effective teaching of reading, therefore, is that which gives the pupil the various skills he needs to make fullest possible use of *context cues* in searching for meaning.'

Extended Beginning Reading (op. cit.) also has a good deal to say about the uses made (or not made) of contextual cues by average readers aged 7 to 9+, for example:

'The use of preceding and succeeding context, and the relevant success in guessing content and function words are also revealing. It is clear that teachers of children in these age-groups need to encourage their pupils to *look ahead* in the text as a means of providing clues to words with which they are experiencing difficulties.'

Additional papers published since 1969 have also explored the theme of contextual cues, for example, Robinson (1972), Goodman, Goodman & Burke (1978), Smith (1980) and Smith (1982).

I am certain that teachers would find any of the publications mentioned to be helpful to them. I hope that they will read some of them, as the theories developed by psycholinguists and others do make sense to me. I am convinced that, when they are put into practice, they enrich reading tuition by widening its scope far beyond the restricted ideas of merely increasing children's sight vocabulary or extending their knowledge of phonic rules.

C Diagnosing children's use of contextual cues

If teachers are to help their pupils to make better use of contextual cues in their reading, more needs to be done than merely encouraging children to 'guess' unknown words. Effective individual guidance needs to be based on diagnostic information. This means that the teacher needs to know the strategies which the child is using or failing to use, when he encounters unknown words. If he is not utilising both the semantic and syntactic cues of the text, then the teacher must take steps to encourage him to do so – and this would probably be best undertaken within a group of children who are similarly handicapped.

The two most commonly used techniques for diagnosing the strategies which individual children are using in their reading are 'Miscue Analysis' and 'Cloze Procedure'. The former is an individual diagnosis, while the latter can be undertaken with a group of children. Both these techniques are based on the belief that when a child deviates from the words in the printed text, during either his silent or oral reading, these deviations, rather than being regarded by the teacher as 'errors', should be looked upon as clues to the strategies he is utilising. When the teacher becomes aware of the strategies he is using to decipher unknown words, she will then be in a position to encourage good strategies and discourage unhelpful strategies.

1   Miscue Analysis

In Miscue Analysis, the teacher chooses a passage of text of about 200 or 250 words, which is at such a level of difficulty for that particular child that he is likely to be unable to recognise a certain number of words, but it should not be so difficult that the child will want to discontinue reading it. The teacher asks the child to read the passage aloud to her and this is tape-recorded. At a later stage, using a duplicated copy of the passage, the teacher enters all deviations from the text and then codes them. (Details of a useful coding system can be found in Chapter 16 of *Extending Beginning Reading* (op. cit.) and in *Listening to Children Reading* (Arnold, 1982).) Once the child's miscues are coded, the teacher can see the exact strategies he is using. Each miscue can be judged in three ways: whether the child is using the grapheme-phoneme* cues (that is the correspondence between the printed symbols and the sounds they represent) in the text correctly; whether his response was syntactically correct – that is grammatically correct; and whether the substituted word was semantically acceptable because it made sense in the context of the passage. The teacher, having diagnosed the child's strategies, is then in a strong position to help him to discard unhelpful strategies and replace them with good strategies. For example, the child whose main tactic, when he is unsure of a word, is to pause and try to puzzle it out from his knowledge of phonic rules, can be encouraged to think more about the meaning of what he is reading and to let his eyes move swiftly ahead to anticipate the sense of the remainder of the sentence. In this way he will be guided to make use also of the semantic and syntactic cues in the text.

*See also the relevant definitions in the Glossary in Appendix 5.

Further helpful advice to teachers on the use of Miscue Analysis as a diagnostic technique can be found in the following two books: Goodacre, *Hearing Children Read* (1979) and Arnold (op. cit.)

2. *Cloze Procedure*

The second method which can be used to assess the strategies children use in their reading, namely Cloze Procedure, has the advantage that it need not be administered individually but can be used with either a group of children or, in the case of older pupils, probably a whole class. A simple introduction to the technique was provided by Moyle (1972) who wrote:

'. . . it is a technique based on the human tendency to complete an incomplete pattern or sequence. Thus if a word is omitted from a sentence the reader attempts to supply the word to complete the meaning.'

Briefly, a passage of prose of suitable length and difficulty for the group in question is selected and words are deleted at regular intervals. The intervals depend on the ages and reading abilities of the pupils to be tested, but the deletion of every tenth word is fairly common. Each pupil is given a duplicated sheet of the passage and asked to read it silently and then to fill in what he thinks the missing words are likely to be. The child's total correct score can provide the teacher with information about the difficulty level of the passage, while the actual words he inserts offer the teacher evidence of his ability to use semantic, syntactic and phonic cues.

In the project *Extending Beginning Reading* (op. cit.) Cloze Procedure was used with groups of from four to eight children of average reading ability, aged 7 to 9+, in order to find out how far these children were successful when forced into using syntactical and semantic cues. In this case, words were not deleted at regular intervals, but selected words were deleted in such a way as to provide the researchers with as much evidence as possible about the child's use of semantic and syntactic cues. Consequently the scoring system was not based on 'correct' or 'incorrect' responses on the basis of the actual words in the original text. Instead the scoring was adjusted to give partial credits for words supplied which were semantically and/or syntactically acceptable in the context of the passage.

It was found that the stage of reading development noted in these average readers of 7–9 years demonstrated a great step forward in their use of a variety of strategies. This stage appeared to be a period of transition in which teachers could greatly help their pupils by encouraging them to approach any difficulty encountered in reading, in an active, problem-solving manner. At this stage, teachers need to encourage their pupils to *look ahead* in the text, as a means of providing clues to words with which they may be experiencing difficulties.

The conclusion drawn at the end of the two chapers on Miscue Analysis and Cloze Procedure, in *Extending Beginning Reading*, was as follows:

'Both Miscue Analysis and Cloze Procedure stem from the same theory of reading – the belief that children should be using all levels of language even in the early stages of learning to read, and that they can be given structured help in doing so.'

Chapters 16 and 17 in the book provide practical guidance on how such help might be given.

IV   Learning to read by reading

Although I have already advocated in this book certain activities which will help children to increase their sight vocabulary, and further activities relating to mastery of phonic rules are suggested in Chapter 6, I should like to emphasise that all these activities and games should occupy only a small proportion of children's time in periods set aside by the teacher for reading. The major portion of children's time, therefore, except possibly in the very earliest stages of beginning reading, should be devoted to *reading* – reading continuous stories, however simple, and other reading material which they are able to read and which they enjoy. I cannot reiterate too strongly how firmly I believe that 'children learn to read by reading' – a phrase used more often nowadays than when I first put it into practice nearly 30 years ago.

Consequently, I firmly endorse the following statement of Smith (op. cit., 1979):

'The implicit knowledge of how to read that all readers have acquired has been developed through reading, and not through exercises or drills. The notion that there are rules that will help children to read completely misses the fact that the only thing that improves reading is practice. Only reading provides the necessary practice in identifying words on sight (not figuring them out letter by letter); in using prior knowledge and context to identify the words and meanings with a minimum of visual information (not struggling blindly and pointlessly to identify one word after another); in predicting, looking for meaning, reading fast rather than slowly, confidently rather than cautiously; in using short-term memory efficiently so that the brain is not overloaded and even the most meaningful of text made nonsense. Most of the "drills" that children are given to help them to read become useful – and easy – only after some skill in reading has been developed.'

Chapter 6

Phonics

I What is meant by phonics?

What do teachers mean when they talk about teaching phonics? They generally mean drawing children's attention to the relationships between single, printed or written letters or groups of letters, and the spoken sounds which the letters usually represent. Thus children are taught that the letter 'P' for example, is usually sounded as in 'pig' or 'pen'. Of course, as English is not a phonetically regular language, because its alphabet consists of only 26 written symbols to represent the 44 sounds in the language, teachers can only *begin* by teaching general rules. This teaching has then to be supplemented – at a fairly early stage – by introducing children to the fact that there are exceptions to many of the regular rules, for example, when the 'p' is followed by 'h', the two letters 'ph' together sound like 'f' – as in 'Philip'.

Two types of approaches to phonic instruction have generally been identified: an analytic and a synthetic method. Definitions of the two approaches can be found in the Glossary in Appendix 5, but put simply the 'analytic' is the 'whole-to-part' method, while the 'synthetic' is the 'part-to-whole' method. To teach children the sound of the digraph 'ee' and then to help them to blend other sounds with it and so build up words, is a synthetic phonic method. To ask children to collect words with 'ee' in them and then to try to read them is an analytical method. (This latter method is the one used in *Sounds and Words* (Southgate & Havenhand, 1979).) Teachers who begin by teaching children phonic rules are, of course, using a synthetic method; although their main aim, as far as reading is concerned, must always be that when their pupils encounter unknown words, they will use their phonic knowledge in an analytical way to help them to break down such words into their phonic components. Consequently, phonic regularities should never be taught in isolation, without reinforcing the learning by encouraging children to spot the relevant letters of components in known words and new words.

II   Decline and resurrection of phonics

The emphasis which has been placed on phonics in the teaching of reading during the nineteenth and twentieth centuries has shown a pattern of fluctuating emphases. To look back on this pattern can be of help to us in appreciating current attitudes to the teaching of phonics. Prior to about 1850, reading tuition was based solely on the alphabetic method; that is by children being taught the names of the letters, 'Ay', 'Bee', 'See' and so on. Gradually, during the middle years of the nineteenth century, phonics were introduced; that is teaching children to say the *sounds* of letters instead of, or in addition to, the *names* of the letters. The twentieth century has seen a varying pattern of the use of phonics in the teaching of beginning reading. Certain periods can be discerned when phonics were predominant, other periods when phonics were in decline and further periods when phonics were being resurrected. These suggested periods, however, are not meant to be regarded as definite and exclusive as, in every case, there has been a great deal of overlap. Consequently, the suggested dates are merely provided as focal points and many years on either side can be regarded as transitional or overlapping periods. It should also be noted that generally more emphasis has been placed on phonics in Scotland and the rest of the United Kingdom than in England.

A   Pre-1945 phonic period

Prior to the 1939–45 war, practically all teaching of beginning reading commenced with phonic training, using a synthetic method; with probably the most well-used reading scheme being *The Beacon Readers* (Grassam, 1922 – and its later editions). The idea of commencing to teach infants to read by training them to recognise discrete words ('look-and-say' method) or whole sentences ('sentence' method), rather than by phonic methods, began to be introduced into teacher-training establishments during the 1930s. Although the first important reading scheme introducing a look-and-say method was published in 1939, namely *Happy Venture Readers* (Schonell & Serjeant, 1939), and a certain number of schools began to use it, the phonic schemes still held sway in the majority of schools until well after the end of the war in 1945.

B   1945–60 Decline in phonic teaching

In the period beginning in 1945 and continuing on into the 1960s, the main strand in reading teaching was closely linked to ₋n increase in the publication of look-and-say reading schemes, some of which were adaptations of schemes originally published in the USA. Look-and-say reading schemes published during this period included *Janet and John** (O'Donnell & Munro, 1949), *Pilot Reading Scheme* (Davenport, 1953), *McKee Readers* (McKee et al., 1956), *The Happy Trio Reading Scheme* (Gray et. al., 1956), *Let's Learn to Read* (Taylor & Ingleby, 1960), *Key Words Reading Scheme** *(Murray, 1964)*, *Queensway Reading* (Brearley & Neilson, 1964), *One, Two, Three and Away!* (McCullagh, 1964), *Ready to Read* (Simpson, 1966) and *Time for Reading* (Obrist & Pickard, 1967). Such schemes were generally much more attractive both in terms of story-line and illustrations than the phonic schemes which they very quickly superseded. Unfortunately, one consequence of this boom in the sale of look-and-say reading schemes was that many teachers who were using them came to believe that it was no longer necessary to draw the attention of their pupils to phonic rules. As a result, in the majority of schools using these schemes, little or no phonic training was undertaken.

However, it would be wrong to suppose that during this period all infant classes switched over to the new look-and-say schemes which were being published. Some schools, through doubts about the efficacy of the newer schemes or through lack of money to launch into the expense of changing reading schemes, continued to teach from schemes already in their schools, of which probably the two most widely used were *The Beacon Readers* (Grassam, 1922, revised editions 1931 and 1957) and *Gay Way Series* (Boyce, 1949), both of which contained phonic components.

The effects of the general movement away from the teaching of phonics began to be noticeable as early as the 1950s. Teachers in junior classes began to complain that pupils being promoted from infant classes were less proficient in reading than they had been five or ten years previously and, furthermore, that the failing readers rarely had any knowledge of phonic rules. During this period, certain local education authorities established remedial reading services to provide extra tuition for failing readers, and many of the remedial teachers concerned quickly realised that *one* of the reasons for these children's low standards of reading was that they had been provided with little, if any, phonic training. Consequently, from about 1955 onwards, remedial teachers, although they still used look-and-say schemes, usually introduced, in addition, some phonic teaching, and a trickle of publications relating to phonics were published towards the end of the 1950s. Among the first of these were *The Royal Road Readers* (Daniels & Diack, 1954) and *Sounds and Words* (Southgate & Havenhand, 1959). The former represented a reading scheme, based on what the authors described as a 'phonic word method', while the latter comprised a set of six supplementary books for pupils, designed to be used alongside any look-and-say scheme. The books contained exercises and activities

---

*The *Janet and John* scheme, although basically a look-and-say scheme, was published in two versions, one of which included some phonic training. *Key Words Reading Scheme* also introduced some phonic training.

intended to be used for five or ten minutes a day, to help children to become familiar with phonic rules and to be able to identify common phonic components within words.

The general procedure in schools, however, up to about 1960 or later, was for the majority of teachers in infant classes to rely on look-and-say reading schemes, paying little, if any, attention to systematic phonic tuition.

C   1960–75 Resurgence of phonics

A 'return to phonics' movement became more noticeable during the 1960s, with additional publications on phonics, in the form of books or apparatus, usually meant to be used as additional materials, alongside look-and-say schemes. These included, *Sound Sense* (Tansley, 1961), *Programmed Reading Kit* (Stott, 1962), *Fun with Phonics* (Reis, 1962), *A Remedial Reading Method* (Moxon, 1962), *Sounds for Reading* (O'Donnell & Munro, 1965) and *Practical Reading: Some New Remedial Techniques* (Webster, 1965). Consequently, during the 1960s and early 1970s, the pattern of reading tuition which tended to become established, particularly with children aged 5 years to about 8 years, was to rely on one or more of the many reading schemes based on a look-an-say method, which were being produced, and to introduce varying amounts of phonic training, using hand-made apparatus or published supplementary materials. (A list of publications relating to phonics is given in Appendix 4.) A number of schools television programmes also introduced phonic training.

In addition, the use of *The Royal Road Readers* (Daniels & Diack, 1954) increased, particularly with older, failing readers, while a more attractive edition of *Gay Way Series* (Boyce, 1959) was published and used by many infant schools.

The picture presented during this period, from approximately 1960 to 1975, was that teachers were becoming much more aware that children not only needed to acquire a large vocabulary of sight words, but that a knowledge of phonics was also necessary as an aid to them in deciphering unknown words. This philosophy was emphasised by the publication of the Bullock Report in 1975 in which it was stated quite clearly that':

> 'Competence in phonics is essential both for attacking unfamiliar words and for fluent reading. The question, then, is not whether or not to teach phonics; of this there can be no doubt. The question is how and when to do it.'

The report itself was in favour of an approach which helped children to learn phoneme-grapheme* correspondences, that is the correspondences between spoken sounds and written symbols, in the context of whole word recognition. It also noted that as the English language has only 26 letters but 44 phonemes, i.e. single letters or groups of letters representing sounds, for example, 'ch', 'th' or 'ough', this causes problems for the child learning to read. (It should be noted that the introduction of the initial teaching alphabet – i.t.a. – for beginning reading, in 1961, provided one means of avoiding this difficulty.)

D 1970–83 Phonics in linguistic approaches

As has already been stated, the suggested periods in the teaching of reading which show different characteristics can only be represented by approximate dates, as there is generally a considerable overlap between one period and another. For example, reading schemes and other reading materials may take five years or more to become widely known and used. Consequently, the resurgence of phonics which was suggested in the preceding period as extending to 1975, overlaps with the emergence of linguistic approaches which commenced about 1970 in England.

Harris & Hodges (*A Dictionary of Reading and Related Terms*, (1981) define a 'linguistic approach or method' as: 'a beginning reading approach based upon regular sound-symbol patterns'. This definition indicates quite clearly that a 'linguistic approach' springs from the same roots as the more old-fashioned term of a 'phonic approach'. Indeed, the earlier linguistic reading schemes which were published in the USA, for example, *Let's Read: A Linguistic Approach* (Bloomfield & Barnhart, 1961) produced sentences at a level of inanity such as 'Can Dan fan Nan?', which is reminiscent of certain of the earlier phonic schemes published in the United Kingdom, and is certainly not the sort of reading material which would currently tempt children to look upon reading as either 'interesting' or 'exciting'.

However, the 1970s and 1980s have witnessed, in the United Kingdom, the publication of a number of reading schemes which do include, to a smaller or greater degree, some emphasis on 'spelling patterns'. These schemes, however, are nothing like the 'Can Dan fan Nan?' type of books, as they usually include, or are based on, stories accompanied by colourful illustrations. Consequently, the phonic element, however small or large, does not detract from children's pleasure. For example, in the teacher's manual for *Language in Action* (Morris, 1974), it is stated that:

' . . . the vocabulary of *Language in Action* has been chosen to highlight a system of spelling pattern progression which is one of its unique features.'

Reading 360 (Clymer, 1978), in its *Activity Books*, provides graded activi-

---

*To be technically correct, when referring to the act of reading, it is the printed symbol (the grapheme) which is the stimulus which should produce the spoken sound (the phoneme). Consequently the phrase should be 'grapheme-phoneme correspondence'. The reverse order of the two words would be appropriate when the child, in his free writing, was trying to spell a word in what he hoped was the correct form.

ties commencing with initial consonants, continuing through the simpler phonic rules and gradually progressing to the learning of common prefixes and suffixes. *Language Patterns* (Moyle, 1981), which is based on 'story method', also includes supporting materials, such as *Working with Letters Books*, *Spelling Books* and *Words and Meaning Books*, in which the spelling patterns of the English language are introduced and practised.

III The place of phonics in reading tuition

I have purposely left this discussion on the place of phonics in a teacher's programme of reading tuition to the penultimate chapter because, from a personal point of view, I do not see it as the first, or most vital, question to be considered. (I should perhaps state that if I were given the choice, I should not select a phonically based reading scheme as the basis for teaching beginning reading.) On the other hand, the fact that *Sounds and Words* (op. cit.) was published at a time when look-and-say methods were in their ascendancy, indicates that I do consider phonics to be one important aspect of reading tuition which we cannot afford to neglect. This is in line with the views of the Bullock Committee, as expressed in the quotation given earlier in this chapter. It is also the general line adopted in the three recently published reading schemes just mentioned. The following points represent a summary of my personal views on the place of phonic training with the total reading programme.

A Not a beginning method

I have four main reasons for believing that phonics should not be used as the main *beginning* method of teaching reading.
They are as follows:

1 English is *not* a phonetic language and, consequently, there are too many exceptions to most phonic rules.
2 I doubt if it is possible to create really interesting and stimulating reading materials for young children by using only those words which are absolutely phonically regular, without also using certain irregular words, such as 'key words to literacy', as well as additional words which have high interest value for young children.
3 Even the earliest reading materials should be, not only meaningful, but of high personal interest to the young child. Consequently, the more quickly children acquire large sight vocabularies of such words, the faster their progress will be and the more enjoyable reading will become to them.
4 Early phonic training instils in children the habit of pausing at each word and trying to decipher it by the application of phonic rules. Yet

fluent reading requires rapid eye-movements across lines of print. For a child to stop at every unknown or doubtful word, to try to puzzle it out, hinders speedy reading and hence his ability to grasp the meaning of sentences and longer passages.

B Some phonic training essential

On the other hand, I consider that some systematic phonic training is not only helpful to children who are learning to read, but that it is essential. The following are the three main benefits to children of having a sound knowledge of phonics or, if one prefers the more recent phraseology, of 'spelling patterns'.

1 To have knowledge of phonic rules can be helpful in contributing to a child's ability to decipher unknown words, when used to confirm or refute 'guesses' or 'predictions' based on other contextual clues relating to the meanings of sentences and larger units.

2 Children in British primary schools spend a great deal of time on 'free' writing. They also take up a large proportion of their teachers' time in making requests of how to spell words. Accordingly, I believe that we should help children to become self-reliant about spelling as quickly as possible. Knowledge of phonic rules will be valuable in this respect.

3 Furthermore, and this is perhaps one of the greatest advantages of phonic training, to be aware of even one phonic rule, almost immediately provides children with a whole batch of new sight words. For example, the rule that when a word begins with 'kn' the 'k' is *always* silent, is a rule which Clymer (1963) described as one with 100 per cent utility, in other words it is an invariable rule. Children thus learn to recognise, in one fell stroke all such words as 'knit', 'knitting', 'knee', kneel', 'kneeling', 'knob', 'knot', 'knife', 'knock', 'knight', 'knave' and so on. Similarly, at a later stage, learning to write and pronounce words ending in ' . . . ture' and ' . . . tion', two other of Clymer's rules with 100 per cent utility, enables children to add a whole list of words to their reading and writing vocabularies, for example, 'picture', 'mixture', 'puncture', and 'action', 'fraction', 'station', 'invitation' and many others.

C Not extensive phonic training

While I believe that some systematic training in phonic rules and elements can be helpful to the majority of children, it seems to me that to insist on an extended, minutely graded phonic programme through which all children must be earnestly pushed or dragged is self-defeating. It becomes a tedious labour which could well quench the pleasure in reading which many beginners will already have experienced by examining and reading many interesting and simple books on their own. As Moon & Raban (*A Question of Reading, 1975*), point out: ' . . . not all children will have difficulty in working out most phonic generalisations for themselves.' They go on to state that any published phonic schemes:

' . . . incorporate a long sequence of steps and stages of complexity from single letters through vowel and consonant combinations to affixes, suffixes and tricky letter clusters like – *ough*. It is therefore tempting to allow children to go through all the steps because that is the way in which the material is structured.'

In contrast, the sensitive teacher will be quite likely to notice, first, children's curiosity about the initial letters of words and she will accept this interest as a starting point and encourage it.

IV Teaching and learning phonics

A Timing the introduction of phonics

Timing the introduction of phonic tuition depends partly on the ages, verbal fluency and past experience of the pupils concerned and partly on the methods and reading materials which the teacher plans to use. Practically all children entering schools at the age of 5 years require a variety of language experiences – for example, talking, listening to stories and rhymes, learning rhymes, examining picture books, labelling the pictures they have drawn or painted, examining labels on objects in the classroom and so on – before any more formal reading programme, whether phonic or look-and-say is introduced. Ongoing activities relating to the objects in the classroom, such as the painting equipment, the shop, the nature-table, the words on children's paintings, pictures and notices throughout the school will have encouraged children to recognise a number of interesting words by sight, as will the activities using children's name-cards, which are outlined in Chapter 3. Indeed it could be these activities involving the children's name-cards which first interest children in the sounds of the initial letters of words.

The book-corners in the classrooms and displays of other simple books will also have afforded children the opportunity to 'read' for themselves such easy books as as *Read it Yourself Books* (Melser, 1960), *This is the Way I Go* (Taylor & Ingleby, 1965), *Methuen Caption Books* (Randell and McDonald, 1968), *First Words* (Southgate, 1968), the earlier levels of *Star Series* (Southgate, 1982) and the simple books listed at Stages 1–3 in *Individual Reading* (Moon & Moon, 1981).

While young children's naturally growing interest in the sounds of letters and the similarity in appearance of words which have the same initial letters should be encouraged in an informal way, any more formal introduction to phonics is best delayed until the following conditions exist:

1 The child has a sight vocabulary of *at least* 100 words;
2 He has shown an interest in the shape and sounds of initial letters in words;
3 He has attended school for at least six months, and in some cases, probably longer;
4 And he has 'read' or enjoyed some of the simple books just listed.

However, in the case of older pupils who have not previously been very successful in reading, and for children in remedial groups, I have found that activities with their name-cards, alongside the opportunity to read simple books which have been very carefully selected so that they will not consider them to be too babyish, provide sufficient background for an early programme of phonics to be introduced.

The timing of the introduction of phonics, of course, also depends on the reading materials to be used. Certain of the newer reading schemes, for example *Reading 360* (op. cit.) and *Language Patterns* (op. cit.) incorporates phonic training within the scheme, usually after a certain amount of look-and-say material has been read. Teachers using such schemes may consider that sufficient phonic training is included in the schemes to obviate the need for additional tuition, although one would hope that incidental reinforcement of phonics would be used by the teacher, whenever opportunities occur in the course of ongoing classroom acitivities.

However, the results of the most recent survey of reading schemes in use in infant schools in Great Britain (Grundin, 1980), based on information gathered in 1978, indicates that the vast majority of infant schools, (as many as 93 per cent, depending on how one classifies a look-and-say scheme) use a look-and-say reading scheme as their principal scheme, and that many of these same schemes are also in regular use as supporting schemes. Consequently it would seem fair to suggest that the majority of teachers of infants, and of slower, older readers, will need to think in terms of phonic training which is either 'incidental' and/or based on published supplementary phonic materials, to be used alongside the many look-and-say reading schemes already in their schools and which they are currently using.

In relation to the timing of the introduction of the more formal type of phonic training, it is interesting to note that, in her book *Stages of Reading Development* (Chall, 1983), Chall hypothesises and presents six stages of reading development, commencing with Stage 0, which she labels, 'Pre-reading: Birth to Age 6'; and that Stage 1, which follows this prereading stage, is described as, 'Initial Reading, or Decoding, Stage: Grades 1–2, Ages 6–7'. In describing this stage, Chall says:

'The essential aspect of Stage 1 is learning the arbitary set of letters and associating these with the corresponding parts of spoken words.'

and,

> 'The qualitative change that occurs at the end of this stage is the insight gained about the nature of the spelling system of the particular alphabet language used.'

Bearing in mind the fact that British children commence school at the age of 5 years, while American children do not begin until the age of 6 years, we can appreciate that the first year of children's reading experience in British schools may be in Chall's terms classified as pre-reading, that is learning to recognise interesting sight words, starting to read the beginning of a look-and-say reading scheme and/or reading simple supplementary books such as those already listed. This implies that by the age of 6 years the majority of children are likely to be ready for some specific, as opposed to incidental, phonic training.

B   Essential phonic skills

1   Sounds and names of letters

Children clearly need to know the sounds of the letters of the alphabet before they can begin to blend them into words and usually this will arise naturally through their perception of identical initial letters in the words on objects, cards, labels and pictures surrounding them. Hughes *(Phonics and the Teaching of Reading,* 1972) shows an interesting pictorial alphabet, which he states 'can assist children in their learning of initial sounds'. The objects in the pictures, for example 'apple', 'banana', 'cat' and 'drum', are each depicted 'in such a way as to represent the shape of its initial letter'. I also think it is helpful if children learn to recognise the shapes of the letters in both upper and lower case, as they go along. The *names* of the letters can be attached to the upper case letters, which enables the teacher to tell children, at a later stage, that although the letter 'S' usually says *s*, sometimes it doesn't as, for example, in 'sugar'. I also find this convention useful in teaching the rule of the 'silent *e*' in monosyllabic words by saying that, 'The "silent *e*" at the end of the word makes the "a" (or other vowel) say its name', for example in such words as 'make', 'these', 'like', 'hope' and 'tube'.

Care needs to be taken in providing young children with the sounds of many of the consonants. For example, *f, l, m, n, r, s* and *v,* can only be pronounced accurately when they are followed by a vowel. Consequently, we must guard against allowing children to say:

fu, lu, mu, nu, ru, su, vu,

(by adding the sound of 'u' to the consonant), instead of merely prolonging the sound of the consonant as:

fff, lll, mmm, nnn, rrr, sss, vvv,

until it is blended with the appropriate vowel or consonant which follows it.

2 Visual and auditory discrimination of letters

Of course, training and practice in visual discrimination between the appearances of letters, and in auditory discrimination between the sounds of letters, is inevitably taking place incidentally in the early infant classes, as children's awareness of the sounds and names of letters is expanding. Even so, all infant teachers use a variety of devices for emphasising these aspects of beginning reading. The teacher, on whose classroom wall I recently saw a *pink* chart covered with pictures and sketches of objects such as, 'pig', 'palace', 'plate', 'pin', 'peas' and 'potato', had clearly been synthesising the children's current interest in the appearance and sound of the initial letter 'p'. She has also been careful not to include words in which the letter 'p' was related to a different sound, such as in 'photograph'.

The game of 'I spy' is frequently used for encouraging auditory discrimination between the sounds of initial letters in words, while rhymes and rhyming games are useful for helping children to focus on the sounds of word-endings. Other activities which teachers can utilise to help children's visual and auditory discrimination are also described in some of the books in Appendix 1, as well as in the publications relating specifically to phonics which are listed in Appendix 4. For the later stage of visual and auditory discrimination, Edwards (1980), in his book *Reading Problems: Identification and Treatment*, Chapters 2 and 3, provides useful lists of games and activities which will help children who have inadequate visual and auditory analysis skills.

3 Blending of letters and sounds

The blending together of an initial consonant and the following vowel in a three-letter word is usually the next stage in phonic training. Indeed the blending is an important stage, for it is often easier for the child to learn to say 'na', 'ne', 'ni', than it is to sound the letter 'n' on its own. In fact the blending together of the sounds of both consonants and vowels in simple three-letter words is an early phonic skill in which children need a good deal of practice – and provision for this was made in the *The Royal Road Readers* (op. cit.) and in *Sounds and Words* (op. cit.), as well as in the many published aids to the teaching of phonics which followed these two publications. Hughes (1979), for instance, provides some useful tips and suggested activities on this and other aspects of phonic training in his book *Using Phonics*.

4   *Syllabification of words*

One of the most important phonic skills, and one which requires specific teaching and practice is the syllabification of words. We help children to learn about phonics in order that they can use these skills to aid them in their deciphering of unknown words. The initial letter of such a word can often give the reader a clue as to what the word might be in the context of the meaning and grammatical structure of the sentence he is reading. But instant recognition of certain clusters of letters which frequently go together to make identifiable portions of words are even more helpful.

I once knew a headmistress who frequently came into the class of 7 year olds whom I was teaching and wrote a very long word on the blackboard, to see which child would be the first to read it. The word might be 'Birmingham', 'Nottingham', 'Workington', 'Mississippi', 'Mr Hetherington', 'conductor', 'understand', 'necessary', 'experiments' or any other word which lent itself easily to syllabification. The children enjoyed puzzling out such words, as they regarded this activity as a challenge. Meanwhile they were learning to recognise common syllables within words and also to lose the hesitancy which many children have about attempting to pronounce lengthy proper nouns, especially people's names and place names which they meet in their books. Spache (1972), in her book, *Reading Activities for Child Involvement*, under a main heading of 'Structural Analysis', suggests many activities to help children to acquire the skills of syllabification by becoming familiar with the roots of words, prefixes, suffixes and so on.

C   Order of introduction of phonic elements and rules

Although different teachers and writers may appear to present somewhat different orders of difficulty for the teaching of phonic elements and rules, in practice there is a very large measure of agreement. The order of presentation is, to a certain extent, dependant upon two features of the English language. First, it is not a regular phonetic language such as, for example, Finnish, in that only 26 letters are available to represent 44 sounds. Consequently we cannot avoid, at a fairly early stage, disclosing to our pupils that 's' or 'o' and other letters sometimes have one sound and sometimes another. Secondly, there are exceptions to many of the common phonic rules. This means that we must provide children with some guidance on the pronunciation of letters and words which do represent exceptions to the general rules. Both these problems are discussed later in this chapter.

Suggested orders of difficulty of phonic elements and rules, which although they demonstrate certain variations, will not be seen to have wide variations, can be found in, among other publications, *The Royal Road Readers* (op. cit.) *Sounds and Words* (op. cit.), and *Programmed Reading*

Kit (Stott, 1962), Chapter 3 of *Roads to Literacy* (Stott, 1964) and Chapter 2 of *Phonics and the Teaching of Reading* (Hughes, 1972).

In any of the suggested orders for the introduction of the phonic components of words, one finds words containing short vowels, single consonants at the beginning and end of words and double consonants such as 'bb', 'nn', 'ss' or 'll', and also 'ck'. Consonant blends at the beginning of words, such as 'sp' and 'st' often come next: followed by consonant blends at the ends of words, for example, 'nd' or 'mp'. Consonant digraphs 'ch' and 'sh' may follow, with 'th', 'wh' and 'qu' being left until later. Of the vowel digraphs, 'ee' and 'oo' are usually introduced fairly early in the programme, with the many other – and more difficult vowel digraphs – such as 'ou', 'ew' and 'ei' being left until later. The rule of the silent 'e' at the end of a word making the preceding vowel say its name (or its 'long sound'), is also usually left until fairly well through the programme. Common endings of words, such as 'ing' and 'ed' may well come earlier, leaving more difficult endings, such as 'tion' and 'ture' for later.

I have found that many of the so-called 'more difficult rules' do not prove as difficult for children to learn as might be anticipated. It seems that, once children acquire 'a mental set' for phonic rules and conventions, they do tend to take the more difficult rules, and exceptions to these rules, in their stride. For example the six remedial teachers who first used *Sounds and Words* (op. cit.) discovered that, as children worked their way systematically through these books, they experienced no greater difficulty in mastering, in Book 6, such rules as 's' sounding like 'sh' in sugar, or ' . . . ous' in 'marvellous' and ' . . . ious' in 'suspicious', than they had done in learning 'sick', 'neck' and 'duck' in Book 1.

It is also probably relevant to note, at this point, that in *Extending Beginning Reading* (op. cit.), when average readers of 7 to 9+ were given a diagnostic phonic test, of the rules tested, the six most difficult phonic elements were found to be, in order of difficulty, as follows:

Category	Item in each category which showed highest failure rate
consonant digraphs	*ph* (as in *Ph*ilip)
silent letters	*b* (as in lam*b*)
word endings	*tion* (as in ac*tion*)
murmur vowels	*ir* (as in s*ir*)
long vowels	*u* (as in t*u*ne)
vowel digraphs	*ou* (as in sh*ou*t)

However, the reasons for children experiencing most difficulties with these particular phonic items may well have been that they had never been systematically taught them, rather than that the categories or particular items themselves were intrinsically difficult. Such a supposition gains credence from the fact that older children (8–9 year olds) exhibited the same pattern of phonic weaknesses as did the younger age-group (7–8 year olds), which strongly suggests that teachers had not diagnosed these weaknesses and set about rectifying them.

D   Mastery of phonic elements and rules

I have always found that children can easily learn the phonic elements and rules of the English language, and will enjoy doing so, provided that the actual teaching sessions are kept quite brief, that is being of no more than five to ten minutes, that the pupils themselves are then actively involved in practice activities and that the teacher consciously reinforces the items currently being learned throughout the day, whenever such opportunities occur.

1   Brief communal introduction to rule

Whatever the phonic element or rule to which the teacher wishes to draw attention at any particular time, it is only rarely that it will be appropriate for a whole class to be involved in the introductory phase of the teaching, although if a teacher suspects that the majority of the class need reinforcement of certain more difficult phonic conventions, a few minutes of oral work together would be appropriate. In general, however, teaching young children to blend together 's' and 'p' at the beginning of words, or, alternatively, the pronunciation of 'ed' and 'ing' at the end of words, is more appropriate for a small group of children.

2   Children collecting examples of words

Once the teacher has introduced her pupils to a new phonic element or rule and helped them to identify the same elements in a number of words which illustrate the rule, one of the best ways I have found of reinforcing the learning is to encourage the children to collect words which display a similar visual element as the one to which their attention has been drawn. Children from the age of about 6 years onward take great pleasure in this activity. It encourages them to be interested in words and to look for similar visual patterns in the words which surround them in books, in school, on the street, in shops, in the home and on television. Children will joyfully bring all the words which exhibit the appropriate visual appearance back to their teacher. Some words will follow the general rule and some will not. Such an activity affords the opportunity for the teacher to help her pupils to understand, quite early in the process of learning to read that, although there exist in the English language many general rules for the pronunciation of written symbols, there are also certain exceptions to these rules. Auditory discrimination can thus be extended alongside visual discrimination.

3 Dealing with exceptions to rules

In Chapter 3 certain activities using children's name-cards were suggested. In the course of these activities, children will soon have spotted that, for instance, a number of the names begin with the letter 'S'. The visual similarity of the initial letters of the names is usually the first thing which children notice. Supposing that there were seven first names which commenced with 'S' under consideration, the teacher might be wise to list the names on the blackboard in the following separate columns:

Sally	Sheila
Sandra	Shaun
Samantha	
Sam	
Stephen	

To have the children read the first list would emphasise that the names all commence with the *sound* of *ss*. Then, listening to the *sounds* of the two names in the second list would show the children that these names did *not* begin with the sound *ss*, as did the other names, but with a different sound of *sh*. By doing this, the teacher will be beginning to make the children aware that, although the letter 'S' *usually* has the sound of *ss*, sometimes it does *not*. If the teacher chooses, at this stage, to draw a ring around the 's' and 'h' in 'Sheila' and 'Shaun', and say the sound *sh*, this could well be the beginning of training in recognising clusters of letters which are frequently found together in words and which represent particular sounds.

Gradually, over a year or two, children will grasp the subtleties of the language and appreciate that although the letter 'S at the beginning of a word is generally sounded *ss*, sometimes it is joined with other letters, as in 'sp . . .', 'st . . .', or 'sm . . ., and that the sounds of two such adjacent consonants should usually be blended together. In the same way 'sh' will become recognised as a unit, whether at the beginning, middle or end of a word, which has to be pronounced in a special way. At a considerably later stage, children will learn that while 'c' at the beginning of a word is generally sounded as *k* in 'cat', sometimes it is sounded like *ss*, for example in 'cigarette', 'circus', 'city', 'centre' and 'circle'. They will also have their attention drawn to the exceptions, such as 'sugar', 'sure' and 'surely', in which the initial letter 's' takes the sound of *sh*.

4 Listing examples

Very soon after children have begun to notice initial letters of words and to equate them with sounds, they will enjoy listing the words they are able to read, in their own word books, as suggested in Chapter 3. Once children have reached a level of phonic proficiency at which they have learned a number of general rules, and are also aware that exceptions to rules sometimes occur, it is a good idea for them to enter all words in which a letter or group of letters does not have the usual sound, and words which exhibit deviations from general rules, in the right-hand columns of their word books, under the title of 'Tricky words'. For example, when children are fully familiar with the *general* rule that a silent 'e' at the end of a monosyllabic word makes the preceding vowel say its name, 'table', 'these', 'mine', 'home' and 'tube' would all be entered in the first column on the appropriate pages. The words 'none' and 'gone' would go in the 'tricky' columns because in these cases the silent 'e' does *not* alter the normal sound of the vowel. Sometimes children find it helpful if the letters which are 'tricky' have a short line drawn under them with a coloured pencil.

If some of these suggested procedures are adoped, after a year or so an 'Ss' page in a child's word book might look as follows.

S s

	Tricky words
Sally	sugar
Sandra	said
Samantha	some
Sam	
Sheila	
Shawn	
sun	
Sunday	
sweets	
soon	
summer	
shop	

It should be noted that if, at an appropriate stage, children are made aware of some of the exceptions to the general phonic rules, this will stand them in good stead when they wish to use their phonic knowledge to provide cues to the pronunciation and meaning of words they do not recognise in running text. For example, the child who first encounters the word 'cinders' in a story may first pronounce it as 'kinders'. If he is reading aloud to his teacher and she says, 'I don't know a word like "kinders" – do you?' They can then explore the possibilities together and one possibility is that 'c' at the beginning of a word is sometimes sounded as *ss* – in the word 'Cinderella' for example. If the child tries the sound *ss* for the letter 'c', he will come up with the correct pronunciation for the word 'cinders'. He can then be trained to check if that makes sense in the context of the sentence and of the story. Thus his interest in words grows and his vocabulary extends.

I must emphasise, however, that this system of children collecting and listing words which they *can* read should not be continued until the children become bored and wearied by it. It is suggested solely as a means of emphasising children's successes and boosting their morale in the early stages of word recognition and the beginning of the mastery of phonic elements in the language. Wisely used, it can be a useful exercise for infants, for older, slower readers and for remedial education. On the other hand, to continue the system too long can become counter-productive. Fluent reading should be the aim of all reading teaching and too long an emphasis on the bits and pieces can delay this end product. Only the teacher can decide when a system has outlived its usefulness and when children are ready to forge ahead without this prop, or to have these first-stage word books replaced by others which are concerned with enlarging their vocabulary of familiar words by the addition of new words of which they know the meanings.

5 Activities for practising sounds, elements, rules and words

Although in Chapters 3 and 4 I have suggested a number of activities and games in which children can be involved in order to increase and consolidate their acquisition of a large sight vocabulary, I have never found it necessary to introduce either hand-made or published apparatus and games as the means of teaching and providing practice for children in phonic rules. Brief group teaching sessions based on the six books of *Sounds and Words* (op. cit.) followed by children's own collections of lists of words, together with training in dealing with exceptions to rules, have always proved effective.

On the other hand, many of both teachers' and pupils' books relating to phonics are now available, as well as a great deal of published apparatus for practising phonics. These are listed in Appendices 1 and 4. Most schools have some of these materials and are using them successfully. A note of caution needs to be added regarding the use of group games, either published or hand-made, for practising phonics. In general such activities are devoid of any checking device. Consequently, either the teacher, or a child who is familiar with the words used in the game, is needed to act as an adjudicator.

E Diagnosis of phonic weaknesses

The effective teacher rarely needs to test her pupils' knowledge of phonic elements and rules during the course of a school year, as her system of teaching, providing practice, checking and recording throughout the year will ensure that she knows exactly which stages groups of pupils and individual pupils have reached. At the beginning of a school year, however, it is useful to be able to give newly promoted pupils a phonic test, the results of which will provide a baseline on which phonic tuition can be established for groups of children with the same needs.

While testing individual children's knowledge of the names and sounds of the letters of the alphabet is theoretically possible, in general the common elements and rules are best tested in the context of words. Furthermore, the words must be 'nonsense words', for the simple reason that we cannot say, for example, that a child who can successfully pronounce the word 'feather', knows the digraph 'th' and the murmur vowel 'er' , or that he is also aware that the vowel digraph 'ea' is, in this case, an exception to the more general rule that 'ea' is pronounced as *ee*. His successful pronunciation of the word may merely represent the fact that the word 'feather' forms part of his sight vocabulary.

Congdon (1974) in his small book *Phonic Skills and their Measurement* provides two extremely useful chapters on phonic testing, including discussions about a number of tests, while Pumfrey's (1976) book *Reading: Tests and Assessment Techniques* represents a valuable source book on all forms of assessment, including phonic tests. Unfortunately, the *Swansea Test of Phonic Skills* (Williams, P. *et al.*, 1971), a test comprising nonsense words is now out of print. Jackson's (1971) *Get Reading Right* is a useful book, in that it not only suggests activities for learning phonics but also includes a number of phonic skills tests. The *Macmillan Diagnostic Reading Pack* (Ames, 1980) consists of a teachers' manual, test cards and individual check lists to provide reading profiles which include the testing of phonic skills within a framework of nonsense words.

Naturally, testing children's phonic capabilities will be followed by recording the results, so that appropriate *ad hoc* teaching and practice groups can be set up. These results should be entered in the teacher's record-book, mentioned in Chapter 2. The categories to be named can be related to the sequence of elements and rules taught and/or tested.

PART FOUR

Organisation of Teachers' and Children's Time

Chapter 7

Organisation of reading time

I The need for effective organisation

Dean & Nichols (1974), in their most helpful book entitled *Framework for Reading*, have this to say about the organisation of work in reading:

> 'Today's teachers are very much in the position of managers of children's learning and it is not irrelevant to consider how efficiently work is going forward. Good organisation demands that teacher and children are using time, space and materials as effectively as possible; that no children are merely "occupied"; that the teacher is not spending a great deal of time on matters which could equally well be dealt with by materials of some kind.'

Every teacher in a primary school has pupils in her class who are at different stages of reading development. This is also true of teachers of remedial reading groups and teachers of slower readers in secondary schools. Consequently, books covering a wide range of difficulty levels are already in every school. These will include more than one reading scheme, as well as a great variety of other books. Practically all schools base their reading tuition on one or more reading schemes. In the most recent survey of the use of reading schemes in use in a sample of infant schools in Great Britain, Grundin (1980), for example, found that:

3 per cent of the schools used *one* scheme only;
11 per cent used *two* schemes;
27 per cent used *three* or *four* schemes;
29 per cent used *five* or *six* schemes;
30 per cent used *seven* or *more* schemes.

Here then is the first large area of organisation – deciding on whether one scheme is the main scheme and others supporting schemes or, alternatively, whether books from the various schemes are to be slotted in at particular levels. Certain schools have already developed master plans for the use of reading schemes, while in other schools head-teachers prefer to allow teachers flexibility in the use of reading schemes.

However, as Dean and Nichols (op. cit.) also point out: 'A school needs a reading programme which is more than a published reading scheme, although this may well be part of it.' Clearly the wider reading programme must be based on more than the simple objective of getting a child through a scheme: it must extend towards the idea of helping every child to become eventually an effective adult reader, one who will go on reading for his personal pleasure and for information, *after* he leaves school, as well as outside the bounds of school while he is still a pupil.

The wider reading programme, of which reading schemes can only form a part, must include diagnostic knowledge of children's mastery or lack of mastery of certain skills as, within each class or group, individual children will have various needs for different kinds and levels of reading tuition. The teacher needs to know the level and kind of tuition required for each pupil and she can only do this if she has diagnosed and recorded whether or not learning has taken place in specific areas. This implies that various materials for assessing reading progress must be available within the school. Teachers must also be aware of all the teaching aids which are available in the form of books, games, equipment such as tape-recorders and teaching machines, and the exact details of what can be taught, practised and learned at different stages by the use of the available reading resources.

Furthermore, the plan for reading tuition will form only part of the total language policy for the school, class and individual. Linking all the different facets of a total language programme for a school, that is the development of listening, talking, reading and writing skills, is far from being an easy task, yet it needs to be carefully considered before plans can be formulated for the effective use of the time and energy of the available human resources, that is the teachers themselves and the parents and/or other helpers whom they are able to recruit.

The successful amalgamation of all these elements represents a mammoth task. Yet I doubt if any teacher chose to train for the teaching profession because she was a capable organiser. The surprising fact is that most teachers have overcome these problems to a certain extent, in that the majority of children do eventually learn to read – although not all pupils are as successful as they might be. How have teachers who were not born organisers achieved this? They have done it by working excessively hard themselves, often at such a pace that they have left themselves insufficient time to ensure that their pupils' time was being utilised in the most fruitful ways, in other words that learning was actually taking place.

For example, in the Schools Council project *Extending Beginning Reading* (op. cit.) it was found that teachers of children aged 7 to 9+ spent a very short amount of time listening to any one child's oral reading due to the many interruptions which caused them to switch their attention constantly from one child to another. It was concluded that little, if any, effective teaching or guidance could be undertaken in such brief contacts between teacher and a pupil. Moreover, the related finding was that this high output of teachers was rarely reflected in high task-orientation in their pupils. Indeed, an obverse effect took over; high teacher output being related to low pupils' output. I am sure that a similar pattern exists in many infant classes.

This particular finding illustrates very clearly the need for teachers to be good organisers. Teachers' thoughts, time and energy need to be planned so that their pupils' time is effectively spent. This involves a continuing programme designed to train children to become as self-reliant as possible – not coming to ask the teacher to help them with every word they cannot read or cannot spell; knowing where to look for the spellings of words they want to write; knowing where to put written work when it is completed; knowing how to record the titles of books they have read on their own, where to replace the books when they have been read and how to choose other books at an appropriate level of difficulty (see *Children who do read* for details of such a system); and being trained to gather up pieces of apparatus, check them and replace them in the appropriate places. Above all, children must be carefully trained about *what to do next*. It is not sufficient for the teacher, at the beginning of a period, to set to work individual children, groups of children or the whole class and then expect that they will all be happily and usefully occupied for half an hour or so. Whatever instruction or guidance is given at the beginning of a period, it always needs to be followed by details of what the children should do when they have finished the set tasks. One method of ensuring this is to have available a large, graded collection of books (see *Children who do read*). When such a system is in operation, children will rarely be found to be engaged in 'non-orientated activities'.

II Class, group and individual activities

A Too much emphasis on individual tuition

During the past 25 years or so, a cult seems to have developed, particularly in infant classes, but also extending to children aged 7 to 9 years, that individual tuition is always best. This trend has been particularly noticeable since the publication of the Plowden Report, *Children and their Primary Schools* (D.E.S., 1966). The persistence of the idea is rather strange because, although the report does note occasions when individual attention is desirable or necessary, it also has something to say about other forms of organisation. For example, the report points out that if all teaching were individual, there would only be seven or eight minutes a day available for every child. It goes on to state:

'Teachers, therefore, have to economise by teaching together a small group of children who are roughly at the same stage. Ideally, they might be better taught individually, but they gain more from a longer period of their teacher's attention, even though it is shared with others, than they would from a few minutes of individual help. This is particularly true of children who have reached the same stage in reading and computation.'

Also, in their final recommendations, the committee did say that, as well as welcoming the trend towards individual learning: 'We recommend a combination of individual, group and class work . . .' The report also suggested that experiments with team teaching might result in 'sets' of pupils from one or two year groups being combined for reading and mathematics according to the stages they had reached.

Even so, in the years which have elapsed since the publication of the Plowden Report, I have only rarely come across group work or cross-classified 'sets' for reading tuition being organised in English primary schools. On the contrary, it has appeared to me that primary school teachers' beliefs in the efficacy of listening to individual children's oral reading, for extremely brief periods of time, continued to increase between 1966 and the publication of the Bullock Report in 1975.

B   Groups of different sizes required

Fortunately, the Bullock Report had this to say about ways of organising reading:

> 'We therefore consider the best method of organising reading to be one where the teacher varies the experience between individual, group and class situations according to the purpose in hand.'

I fully endorse this statement, although teachers will need to consider carefully the kinds of activities in the field of language and reading which are best suited to groups of varying sizes. The following are suggestions of some of the kinds of activities which teachers might find best suited to class, group and individual situations, as far as learning to read is concerned. Certain of these proposals were put forward in *Extending Beginning Reading* (op. cit.), while others relate to activities already mentioned in this book and in *Children who do read*.

1   Class activities

(a) The teacher reads aloud a story to the class or shares with the children something she herself has enjoyed reading, whether it is part of a book, articles from newspapers and magazines, letters or any other written materials she thinks will interest her pupils.

(b) The whole class is provided with increasingly lengthy periods when every child in the class is reading silently, without any interruption, books of their own choice, from a graded selection of books. (This practice is described fully in *Children who do read*.) In relation to these two points it is worth noting that in the project *Extending Beginning Reading* (op. cit.) teachers of 7 to 9 year olds spent much more time in reading aloud to their pupils, to stimulate their interest in books with a view to encouraging them to do more personal reading, than the time they allowed the children for personal reading, that is to satisfy the interests they were trying to arouse and to ensure that the habit of reading became established. The reverse, of course should be the case.

(c) A session devoted to a 'sharing' of books can be enjoyed, if children bring their favourite books from home and spread them around the room. Everyone samples the books for a short while and then all settle down with chosen books. Finally, a few children might like to tell the class about the books they have examined or read.

(d) Children aged 6 years and upwards can begin preliminary training in the order of the letters of the alphabet, by being introduced to very brief communal activities and games, as a class activity. (See Book 3 in this series, entitled *Reading for information*.)

(e) At a later stage, the beginning of training in the use of dictionaries can take the form of brief class activity sessions. (This is also described in Book 3.)

(f) Discovery by the teacher that all or most of the children in the class are uncertain of a particular phonic rule or about exceptions to rules may call for a short session of class activities.

(g) Vocabulary extension sometimes arises spontaneously, when a particular child discovers a new word, and this results in the teacher gathering together the attention of the whole class for a minute or two, to discuss the meaning of the word and to consider synonyms or opposites.

2 Group activities

(a) Infants, and also older children, whose reading tuition is based on a reading scheme, are frequently divided into reading groups according to the stage they have reached in the reading scheme. I have found that the best way of working with any such group is for the teacher to sit at her own table, facing the remainder of the class who are engaged in prescribed reading tasks. The children in the group stand around the table, each with his book laid open on the table in front of him. The teacher is then in a position to keep an eye on the rest of the class, who should have been trained not to disturb her while she is so engaged, at the same time as she is engaged in working with the group at her table. The group can read a whole story with the teacher, taking it in turn to read aloud, discussing difficulties, talking about the meanings of new words, the characters in the story and the ideas behind it. The group discussion will help the teacher to be sure that the children have understood what they have been reading and to have the opportunity of encouraging them to bring their own experiences to bear on the story. It will provide opportunities for vocabulary extension and for diagnosis of individual weaknesses as one child reveals a gap in his knowledge of words, which others will try to help him to rectify.

For the teacher to work with a group in this way also affords her the opportunity to encourage the children to predict what unknown words might be, by utilising contextual clues as meaningful pointers. Similar training to concentrate on the meaning of what her pupils are reading can be provided by asking children to predict how the story will end and then questioning them as to what made them reach this conclusion.

Ten minutes spent with six or eight children in this way can be much more fruitful than one minute spent with each child individually. It is a sociable as well a teaching–learning occasion and, having participated in it, the children concerned will usually return happily to their seats and be content to continue quietly with follow-up reading activities prescribed by their teacher.

(b) As already mentioned earlier in this book, when a teacher discovers that a number of children in the class have not mastered, for example, a phonic rule or the first 100 words in *Key Words to Literacy* (op. cit.) this is the occasion to gather those particular children into an *ad hoc* group and teach the skill which is lacking. The same group can then be directed to group activities in the form of games, for practising the skill before it is retested.

(c) It is also a useful activity for children who are at the same stage of being about half-way through an infant reading scheme or using the later books or extension readers in a scheme, to read together in a group. Children aged about 7 years and older are usually gregarious creatures and enjoy such a group activity, which also provides them with practice in fluent oral reading. If children are properly trained for this, they will be able to do it in one corner of the room when the remainder of the class are engaged in quieter activities, or in an area outside the classroom. The first essential feature of such group reading is that children should not have to wait a long time for their 'turn' to read. Consequently, three or four children would be an appropriate size for such a group. The books chosen should be within the children's capacity, so that they only rarely meet unknown words. Consequently, the oral reading will be fluent rather than halting. The type of slim books which are intended as 'platform readers' or 'supplementary books' to reading schemes often prove suitable for such oral group reading sessions.

A leader should be appointed *for that session only*. Children will take it in turn to act as leaders on succeeding occasions. The leader will name each child in turn who is to read and will allow him to read only one paragraph at a time – and will never stop the child who is reading in the middle of a sentence. If the reader meets a word he doesn't recognise and no one else in the group knows it, the leader will write it down. At the end of the session, the teacher will spend a minute or so with the group, asking them about the story and helping with any difficult words encountered.

(d) Practice activities in the form of games which a group of children can play in order to reinforce recently learned sight-words or phonic conventions form one of the most popular, as well as useful, group activities. Examples of such games and activities are given in Chapters 3 and 4 of this book, together with suggestions of ways of ensuring that the children behave in an orderly and prescribed manner, so that the games do not prove to be a disturbance to ther children in the room. (Appendix 1 lists publications relating to many practice games.)

One important point to stress in using both published and hand-made reading games is that each school should set up its own classification system, so that the staff are aware of the skill or skills for which each game is designed to provide practice. Dean & Nichols (op. cit.) for example, suggest that symbols should be allocated to each separate section, such as a square for phonic work and a diamond for word recognition.

3 Individual activities

Most children in primary schools appreciate having the opportunity, at some point in the day, to choose what they will do. In infant schools their choices will show great variety and mostly the activities chosen will be those involving physical activities. Even so, some children will choose to examine books or to read them. But occasions for working individually in reading and language periods also need to be offered as part of a full language programme. Such times will afford the child opportunities to read different books from the usual ones, to write about what they have read, to collect lists of words or to practise particular skills. Frequently the individual activities will entail the child working entirely on his own, while at other times he will be having the individual attention of his own teacher or a parent helper. The following examples show some of the forms which individual activities or individual attention could take.

(a) Individual children working on their own
(i) The time set aside every day for children to read their self-selected books without interruptions, while in one sense a class activity is, as far as the child himself is concerned, also an individual activity.

(ii) Practising, in the manner prescribed in Chapter 3, with a small pack of cards, each showing a single word, whether the packs be 'interesting words' or 'key words', provides children with an extremely useful individual activity for increasing their sight vocabulary.

(iii) 'Collecting' words which commence with the same sounds, or words which follow certain phonic rules, or undertaking very brief phonic exercises, such as some of those suggested as follow-up activities in *Sounds and Words* (op. cit.), also provide worth-while activities which children enjoy undertaking individually.

(iv) Collecting rhyming words from books of rhymes or poems reinforces the learning of groups of letters forming word endings.

(v) Making short words from long words is another enjoyable and useful individual activity. For example: 'See how many different words you can make, using only the letters in "Constantinople".'

(vi) There are also vast quantities of published apparatus which children can use individually for practising certain skills. If a child is to use such apparatus on his own, it must fulfil three criteria: first, it must be self-checking; secondly the instructions must be sufficiently clear for the child to read and understand or, alternatively, he must have been trained to use it; and thirdly the game or apparatus must be kept in a particular place under a group label or symbol, from which the child knows that he may select materials.

(vii) Simple books, each containing one short story or a few rhymes can be recorded on tape. The child who wants to read a particular book can then listen to the taped voice reading the story, while he follows the words in the text.

(viii) Individual children can illustrate a story they have read and then write about it.

(ix) At a later stage, individual children who have enjoyed a particular book may like to produce a poster about it for the notice board, make an attractive book cover for it or write up a book report, which will go in a specified box or ring file, which other children can consult. Special book report forms may be duplicated and kept in a box for children to use when they feel the urge to do so. These book report forms or cards should each contain spaces for the name of the author of the book, its title and the name of the reporter. A large space could be headed by a phrase such as 'This book is about . . .', while there might be a further space headed, 'The things I liked best about this book were . . .'.

(b) *The teacher working with an individual child*
In the research project *Extending Beginning Reading* (op. cit.), it was found that the average 30 seconds which a teacher devoted to a individual child was totally inadequate for diagnosing his weaknesses, evaluating his understanding of what he had read or probing the strategies he was using. Consequently, it was suggested that teachers should restructure their system of using oral reading periods by extending the period which they spent with an individual child, but that such a period would be required less frequently. With children aged 6–7 years such periods could begin with five minutes, while with older pupils the periods could later be extended to ten minutes or so. The following were the suggestions made in the report of some of the things which might be undertaken in different individual sessions, with children aged 7 to 9+ :

'(i) The child reading aloud a few pages from a self-chosen book;
(ii) Discussion of the content of the book, reasons why it was chosen, the child's particular interests and hobbies related to books, and how he sets about finding books which interest him;

(iii) Probing his comprehension of what he is reading – not just literal comprehension;
(iv) Checking whether or not he recognises the first 200 *Key Words to Literacy*;
(v) Administering a diagnostic test of his phonic competencies;
(vi) Vocabulary extension, in the context of his reading;
(vii) Carrying out a miscue analysis of the errors he makes in oral reading, with a view to discovering the strategies he is using;
(viii) Encouraging him to use knowledge of the meaning of words, the sense of phrases and sentences and the normal grammatical structure of the English prose to provide cues to words or phrases he does not recognise;
(ix) Keeping notes, records, tape-recording, etc. of these sessions and thereby gradually building up a comprehensive file of his reading and its progress;
(x) Examining and discussing with the child his record of books he has read in the preceding few weeks and comments, reviews, etc. he may have written;
(xi) Planning, with the child's help, the course of his reading activities for the succeeding few weeks.'

Arnold's (1982) book, *Listening to Children Reading* will also be found helpful in planning this kind of contact with individual children, especially in respect of probing children's use of contextual cues.

III The total organisational plan

To organise a complex reading programme, involving class activities, group activities and individual activities, is by no means simple and I should certainly not consider advocating a blueprint which would be effective for every teacher in every school. There are too many factors involved in the situation to do this, not least of which are the size of the school, the ratio of staff to pupils, the aims and beliefs of the head-teacher and his or her staff, their preferred modes of working, the number and qualifications* of voluntary helpers and the materials and equipment available.

If the staff of a school consider introducing, extending or altering their overall reading plan for the school, they might find it helpful to read the following three books:

Framework for Reading (Dean & Nichols, 1974), with particular reference to Chapter 7, 'The Organisation of Work in Reading';
Independence in Reading (Holdaway, 1980), with particular reference to the chapter entitled 'The Individualised Reading Programme';
Listening to Children Reading (Arnold, 1982), with particular reference to Chapter 6, 'The Organisation of Reading Aloud for Different Purposes'.

---

*e.g. Some of the voluntary helpers may be mothers who had originally trained as teachers, while others may be retired teachers.

This should be followed by full and free staff discussions, until a consensus of opinion emerges.

I would suggest that any ambition to put a new total organisational plan into effect, at one stroke, should be avoided. It would be preferable to devise a tentative plan and to follow that by deciding on the various stages in which it would be introduced, over a fairly extended period of a year or two. For example, it might be decided that the first stage could be to undertake a comprehensive reorganisation of all the reading apparatus and equipment in the school, with a view to categorising, storing and labelling it, so that every teacher could have a complete list of all that was available, and eventually children could be trained to take what was needed and return it to the same place.

Alternatively, or in addition, a reorganisation and grading of many of the books in the school, possibly excluding reading schemes, could be undertaken – as spelt out in great detail in *Children who do read*. (Suggestions are also provided in this book of ways in which parents could help with this task.)

IV   The use of voluntary helpers

A further preliminary point to be considered is how parents or other voluntary helpers might best be recruited, to undertake certain of the necessary tasks within the new overall plan: followed by decisions on which tasks such helpers might or might not undertake. Clearly the introduction of the youngest pupils to their first books is a task for the teacher, as is the diagnosis of difficulties, record-keeping and promotion of pupils from one reading stage to the next. On the other hand, for teachers to spend hours in making apparatus or labelling apparatus and books is a complete waste of their expertise. The teachers are the people qualified to categorise and grade both books and equipment, while helpers can do the labelling and so on. Parents can keep the apparatus and books in good repair, make apparatus and help to train young children to put it away. They can read stories to children and they can listen to individual children in a group reading aloud, once they have been trained exactly what to do if a child does not recognise a word. They can discuss the stories which have been read with the children. Duplicating materials, preparing packets or boxes for equipment, preparing and sticking up posters, setting up book exhibitions, organising book clubs and helping to run the library are all tasks with which voluntary helpers can become involved, if teachers are only willing to welcome them into their schools and initiate them into undertaking various tasks.

V   The reading atmosphere

In British primary schools we find a much more informal approach to the teaching of reading and learning to read than can be seen in certain other countries, for example the USA and Canada, where the teaching is usually based on very substantial basal reading schemes, which the teachers follow quite closely, according to the definite instructions set out in detailed teachers' manuals. I have noted, in these countries, that when teachers follow meticulously these copious teachers' instructions relating to such substantial schemes, the task of learning to read tends to become such an earnest business that there is little time for considering or experiencing the delights of reading.

In contrast, in practically all primary schools in the United Kingdom, the emphasis is on the pleasures of reading. Motivation is considered of prime importance, children are encouraged to handle books freely, to browse among wide selections of books and to have opportunities to examine books and to try to read personally selected books. Formal instruction is usually reduced to a minimum. Such regimes are designed to produce children who will become real readers rather than children and adults who will merely be able to read when the necessity arises.

However, it would be wrong to think that the informal way of encouraging reading is the easiest method for teachers to follow. On the contrary, such a teacher has a much more difficult role to play than that of the reading instructor who carefully follows the guidelines laid down by someone else for the use of a comprehensive basal reading scheme. The more informal regimes existing in most of our primary schools represent a much more difficult task for the teachers concerned – a tiring, but clearly satisfying task, which the teachers cheerfully undertake. British teachers are eager to help children to learn to read so that they may share with them the pleasures of reading, but the happy and relaxed reading atmosphere to be observed in the schools has not been achieved without a great deal of behind-the-scenes thought and hard work on behalf of the teachers concerned. I am convinced, however, that such regimes are more likely to encourage children to want to read outside school and to go on reading when they eventually leave school than are the entirely formal reading programmes, meticulously followed.

I believe that the *habit* of reading as a pleasurable and absorbing activity should be established early and continue throughout the years of schooling. It is for this reason that the first book in this series of three books, under the title of *Planning For Reading Success* has the title of *Children who do read*, and it deals entirely with ways of ensuring that the larger part of any reading programme is just that – individual, silent reading of self-selected books.

The two contrasting attitudes to reading are well illustrated by the following quotations from children involved in the research project *Extending Beginning Reading* (op. cit.). When 8 and 9 year olds were asked 'Do you think children should learn to read?', one boy saw the usefulness of learning to read '. . . and then you can stop.' Another saw the need for knowing how to read because he would need the skill for the harder work he would have to do at the secondary school stage. In contrast, a 9-year-old boy, when asked if he preferred to read aloud to someone or to read quietly to himself, answered in this way:

> 'To myself. If you say the words wrong it's easier to yourself. You don't have to stop to get breath. I lose myself in it. I get away from the rest of the class in my head. I work myself into the book.'

This last boy was already a *real* reader and I doubt if this would have been so had he not been given plenty of opportunities for reading personally selected books at appropriate levels of difficulty. Yes, we do need to help children to learn *how* to read, but the time devoted to the careful training suggested in this book need only represent a minor portion of the reading programme, as long as it is regularly undertaken as part of a systematic plan. Let the major part of the reading programme be along the lines proposed in *Children who do read* and a minor, although vital part, related to the activities outlined in *Reading: Teaching for learning*.

Appendix 1: Books describing games and activities for practice in word recognition

Ames, T. (1983) *40 Remedial Games to Make and Play* (London: Macmillan Education)

Burns, P. C. & Roe B. D. (1900) *Reading Activities for Today's Elementary Schools* (Chicago: Rand McNally College Publishing Company)

California Reading Association (1970) *Fresh Ideas for Teaching Reading.* Obtainable from California Reading Association, 3400 Irvine Avenue, Suite 211, Newport Beach, California 92660, USA

Hall, N. A. (1969) *Rescue: A Handbook of Remedial Reading Techniques for the Classroom Teacher.* Obtainable from Educational Service Inc., PO Box 219, Stevensville, Michigan 49127, USA

Herr, S. E. (1961) *Learning Activities for Reading* (Dubuque, Iowa, USA: William C. Brown Company Publishers)

Hughes, J. M. (1970) *Aids to Reading* (London: Evans)

Hughes, J. M. (1972) *Phonics and the Teaching of Reading* (London: Evans)

Hughes, J. M. (1979) *Using Phonics* (London: Macmillan)

Jackson, S. (1971) *Get Reading Right* (Glasgow: Bissett and Son)

Platts, M. E., *et al.* (1960) *SPICE: Suggested Activities to Motivate the Teaching of the Language Arts in the Elementary School.* Obtainable from Educational Service Inc., PO Box 219, Stevensville, Michigan 49127, USA

Root, B. (1982) *40 Reading Games to Make and Play* (London: Macmillan Education)

Russell, D. H. & Karp, E. E. (1959) *Reading Aids through the Grades.* Obtainable from Bureau of Publications, Teachers College, Columbia University, New York, USA

Southgate, V. & Havenhand, J. (1979) *Sounds and Words* (London: Hodder and Stoughton)

Spache, E. B. (1972) *Reading Activities for Child Involvement* (Boston: Allyn and Bacon)

Appendix 2: Suppliers of equipment

Centre for the Teaching of Reading, University of Reading School of Education, 29 Eastern Avenue, Reading, RG1 5RU

Suppliers of *Resources for Teaching Phonics: Annotated Lists of Games, Tests, Tapes, Books and Teaching Aids* (Roots, B., 1982) and *Reading Skill Acquisition: Comparative Lists of Reading Games and Support Materials* (Raban, B., 1982)

Holmes McDougall Limited, Allander House, 137 Leith Walk, Edinburgh EH6 8NS

Suppliers of phonic apparatus and games in the form of: *Programmed Reading Kit* (Stott, D., 1966) and *Letter-Link Kits* 1–3 (Reid, J. and Donaldson, M., 1978–80)

James Galt and Company Limited (Education Division), Brookfield Road, Cheadle, Cheshire SK8 2PN

Suppliers of *Key Words Lotto* 1, 2, and 3, and for other cards and board games relating to 'sight words' and phonic skills

Ladybird Books Limited, Loughborough, Leicestershire

Suppliers of *Ladybird Flashcards* and *Ladybird Reading Games Box* – both relating to *Key Words to Literacy*

Schoolmaster Publishing Company Limited, Derbyshire House, St Chad's Street, London WC1

Suppliers of *Key Words Attainment and Diagnostic Test* devised by J. McNally, and also of *Key Words to Literacy and the Teaching of Reading* by J.McNally and W. Murray (1971), which describes certain games that children can play in order to practise 'key words'

Appendix 3: Suggested sheets for recording children's mastery of 'Key Words to Literacy'

Name...Class.....................Tester.................

Dates of Testing...

FIRST 100 WORDS

Pack 1

is
the
a
he
it
of
in
and
I
that
to
was

Pack 2

but	at
we	his
so	be
as	one
not	they
had	you
on	are
with	for
him	all
said	have

Pack 3(a)

an	up
she	look
no	get
old	has
big	will
me	then
out	her
can	did
them	my
if	little
or	went
like	

Pack 3(b)

been	when
well	two
this	were
go	by
must	much
make	made
see	call
off	do
now	which
into	over
back	your
from	

Pack 3(c)

new	some
other	our
who	down
before	here
what	about
come	more
there	their
came	first
only	where
want	right
could	just

SECOND 100 (+1) WORDS

Pack 4(a)

ran	dog
run	got
put	ask
sit	bad
sat	too
am	good
let	soon
red	room
man	keep
men	tree
yes	green
tell	three
fell	

Pack 4(b)

saw	black
us	blue
four	fly
five	boy
help	girl
eat	bird
read	stop
say	fast
may	last
day	best
play	hand
away	work
take	

Pack 4(c)

sing	gave
bring	long
thing	jump
think	Mr
than	Mrs
give	father
live	mother
once	woman
after	find
school	found
wish	round
time	how
never	very

Pack 4(d)

walk	again
any	own
would	know
should	always
next	head
every	white
because	left
open	another
don't	why
going	under
many	these
home	year
house	

50 (−1) ADDITIONAL NOUNS

	Pack 5(a)		Pack 5(b)	

Pack 5(a)		Pack 5(b)	
bag	ball	apple	children
bed	tea	cow	place
box	sea	money	train
egg	toy	letter	road
top	doll	end	sister
sun	shop	street	picture
pig	book	table	rabbit
jam	fish	door	horse
cat	car	name	farm
hat	baby	dinner	nothing
bus	milk	night	today
fund	hill	morning	water
cup			

N.B. The word 'Mrs' has been moved from '50 Additional Nouns' and placed beside 'Mr' in Pack 4(c), as it is easier for children to learn these two abbreviations at the same time.

Appendix 4: Publications relating to phonic training

Ames, T. (1980) *The Macmillan Diagnostic Reading Pack* (London: Macmillan)

Chall, J. S. (1967) *Learning to Read: The Great Debate* (New York: McGraw-Hill)

Clymer, T. (1963) 'The Utility of Phonic Generalisations' (*The Reading Teacher*, 16, 4, 252–258)

Congdon, P. J. (1974) *Phonic Skills and their Measurement* (Oxford: Basil Blackwell)

Daniels, J. C. & Diack, H. M. A. (1954) *The Royal Road Readers* (London: Chatto and Windus)

Edwards, P. (1980) *Reading Problems: Identification and Treatment*, Chapters 3 and 4 (London: Heinemann Education Books)

Harris, A. J. & Sipay, E .R. (1975) (6th Edition) *How to Increase Reading Ability*, Chapters 14 and 15 (New York: David McKay)

Hughes, J. M. (1970) *Aids to Reading* (London: Evans)

Hughes, J. M. (1972) *Phonics and the Teaching of Reading* (London: Evans)

Hughes, J. M. (1971) *Using Phonics* (London: Macmillan)

Jackson, S. (1971) *Get Reading Right* (Glasgow: Bissett and Son)

Obrist, C. (1972) *Time for Sounds*, Books 1–6 (Aylesbury: Ginn)

Reid, J. & Donaldson, M. (1978–80) *Letter-Link Kits 1–3* (Edinburgh: Holmes McDougall)

Root, B. (1982) *Resources for Teaching Phonics: Annotated Lists of Games, Tests, Tapes, Books and Teaching Aids* (Reading: Centre for the Teaching of Reading, University of Reading)

Southgate, V. and Havenhand, J. (1979) *Sounds and Words*, Books 1–6 and Teachers' Manual (London: Hodder and Stoughton)

Spache, E. B. (1972) *Reading Activities for Child Involvement*, Chapter 4 (Boston: Allyn and Bacon)

Stott, D. H. (1962) *Programmed Reading Kit* (Glasgow: Holmes)

Stott, D. H. (1964) *Roads to Literacy* (Glasgow: Holmes)

Tansley, A. E. (1961) *Sound Sense* (Leeds: Arnold)

Tansley, A. E. (1972) *Reading and Remedial Reading*, Chapters 5 and 6 (London: Routledge and Kegan Paul)

Appendix 5: Glossary*

analytic phonics, a whole-to-part phonics approach to reading instruction in which the student learns a number of key sight words, is taught the relevant phonic generalisations, and applies these generalisations to particular examples in learning symbol–sound correspondences; deductive phonics. (Contrast – *synthetic phonics*.)

cloze procedure any of several ways of measuring a person's ability to restore omitted portions of an oral or written message from its remaining context. *Note:* W. Taylor coined the term 'cloze' in 1953 to reflect the Gestalt principle of 'closure', the ability to complete an incomplete stimulus. In reading practice, a standardised procedure and set of scores have been developed to differentiate frustration/instructional reading levels and instructional/independent reading levels.

consonant digraph, a combination of consonant letters representing a single speech sound as 'gn' for /n/ in 'gnat', or 'gh' for /f/ in 'rough'.

content word, a word having lexical meaning as 'cat', 'duty', 'house'. (Contrast – *function word*.)

digraph, *n.* two letters which represent one speech sound, as 'ch' for /ch/ in 'chin'.

function word, a type of word that has a grammatical, but not a lexical meaning, as in 'the', 'or'. (Contrast – *content word*.)

grapheme, *n.* a written or printed orthographic representation of a phoneme, as 'b' and 'oy' for /b/ and /oi/ in 'boy'. *Note:* In English, a grapheme may be a single alphabet letter or a group of letters as in 'boy' above, and includes all the ways in which it may be written or printed.

grapheme-phoneme correspondence the relationship between a grapheme and the phoneme(s) it represents; letter–sound correspondence, as 'c' representing /k/ in 'cat' and /s/ in 'cent'. *Phonics as a teaching device concerns grapheme-phoneme correspondences: how to pronounce words when seen in print. Note:* Technically, grapheme-phoneme correspondence refers to letter-to-sound correspondence, not vice versa. (Contrast – *phoneme-grapheme correspondence*.)

*N.B. The definitions in this glossary are taken from: Harris, T. L. & Hodges, R. E. (eds), 1981, *A Dictionary of Reading and Related Terms*. (In certain cases, in the interests of simplicity, not all the details provided in the definitions have been included.)

linguistic approach, *or* **method** 1 any approach to the teaching of reading based upon linguistic principles; 2 a beginning reading approach based upon regular sound-symbol patterns, first proposed by Neef in 1913 and more recently by L. Bloomfield in the 1930s. *Note:* The terms 'linguistic approach', 'method' or 'program' have been used to refer to so many different kinds of linguistic content as to be virtually meaningless.

linguistics, *n.* the study of the nature and structure of language and languages.

miscue, *n.* an oral reading response that differs from the expected response to the written text. *Note:* Miscues are an interaction between the reader's grammatical system, experience, and the printed page just as are accurate reading responses. For this reason, K. Goodman and his associates believe miscues reflect the strengths and weaknesses of the reading strategy of the reader. Thus an analysis of the miscues of individuals may provide information for planning reading instruction.

phoneme, *n.* a minimal linguistic unit in spoken language whose replacement can result in a meaning difference, as /p/, /b/ in 'pin', 'bin'.

phonics, *n.* an approach to the teaching of reading and spelling that stresses symbol–sound relationships, especially in beginning reading instruction.

phoneme-grapheme correspondence, the relationship between a phoneme and its graphemic representation(s), as /s/. spelled 's' in 'sit', 'c' in 'city', 'ss' in 'grass'. *Note:* Technically phoneme-grapheme correspondence refers to sound-to-letter correspondence, not vice versa. (Contrast – *grapheme-phoneme correspondence.*)

psycholinguistics, *n.* the interdisciplinary field of psychology and linguistics in which language behaviour is examined.

semantic cue, evidence from the general sense or meaning of a written or spoken communication that aids in the identification of an unknown word. (Compare – *syntactic cue.*)

syntactic cue, evidence from a knowledge of the rules and patterns of language that aids in the indentification of an unknown word from the way it is used. (Compare – *semantic cue.*)

synthetic phonics, a part-to-whole phonics approach to reading instruction in which the student learns the sounds represented by letters and letter combinations, blends these sounds together to pronounce words, and is taught the phonic generalisations that apply in learning symbol–sound correspondences; inductive phonics. (Contrast – *analytic phonics.*)

tachistoscope, *n.* any mechanical device for the controlled and usually very brief exposure of visual materials, as pictures, words, phrases and sentences.

vowel digraph, a spelling pattern in which two or more adjoining letters represent a single vowel sound, as 'eigh' for /ā/ in 'sleigh', 'ea' for /e/ in 'bread' or 'aw' for /ô/ in 'saw'.

References

Ames, T. (1980) *The Macmillan Diagnostic Reading Pack* (London: Macmillan)

Ames, T. (1983) *40 Remedial Games to Make and Play* (London: Macmillan Education)

Anderson, I. H. & Dearborn, W. F. (1952) *The Psychology of Teaching Reading* (New York: The Ronald Press)

Arnold, H. (1982) *Listening to Children Reading* (London: Hodder and Stoughton)

Bloomfield, L. and Barnhart, C. L. (1961) *Let's Read: A Linguistic Approach* (Detroit: Wayne State University Press)

Boyce, E. R. (1949 – revised 1966) *Gay Way Series* (London: Macmillan)

Brearley, M. & Neilson, L. (1964) *Queensway Reading* (London: Evans)

Burns, P. C. & Roe, B. D. (1979) *Reading Activities for Today's Elementary Schools* (Chicago: Rand McNally's College Publishing Company)

California Reading Association (1970) *Fresh Ideas for Teaching Reading.* Obtainable from California Reading Association, 3400 Irvine Avenue, Suite 211, Newport Beach, California 92660, USA

Centre for the Teaching of Reading, University of Reading (1980) *Reading Resources*

Ceprano, M. A. (1981) 'A review of selected research on methods of teaching sight words' *The Reading Teacher*, 35, 3, 314-22

Chall, J. S. (1967) *Learning to Read: The Great Debate* (New York: McGraw-Hill)

Chall, J. S. (1983) *Stages of Reading Development* (New York: McGraw-Hill)

Congdon, P. J. (1974) *Phonic Skills and their Measurement* (Oxford: Basil Blackwell)

Clymer, T. (1963) 'The Utility of Phonic Generalisations' *The Reading Teacher*, 16, 4, 252-88

Clymer, T. (ed.) (1978) *Reading 360* (Aylesbury: Ginn)

Daniels, J. C. & Diack, H. M. A. (1954) *The Royal Road Readers* (London: Chatto and Windus)

Davenport, P. (1953) *Pilot Reading Scheme* (Leeds: E. J. Arnold)

Dean, J. & Nichols, R. (1974) *Framework for Reading* (London: Evans)

Department of Education & Science (1967) *Children and Their Primary Schools Vol. 1* Plowden Report (London: H. M. Stationery Office)

Department of Education & Science (1975) *A Language for Life,* Bullock Report (London: H. M. Stationery Office)

Dolch, E. W. (1943) 'Basic Sight Vocabulary of 220 Words' *A Manual For Remedial Reading* (Champaign, Illinois, USA: Garrard Press)

Edwards, P. (1980) *Reading Problems: Identification and Treatment* (London: Heinemann Educational Books)

Fowler, H. W. & Fowler, F. G. (5th edition 1964) *The Concise Oxford Dictionary of Current Usage* (Oxford: Clarendon Press)

Goddard, N. L. (1969) *Reading in the Modern Infants' School* (London: University of London Press)

Goodacre, E. (1979) *Hearing Children Read* (Reading: Centre for the Teaching of Reading, University of Reading)

Goodman, K. S., Goodman, Y. M. & Burke, C. (1978) 'Reading for Life: The Psycholinguistic Base' in Hunter-Grundin, E. & Grundin, H. U. (eds) *Reading: Implementing The Bullock Report* (London: Ward Lock Educational)

Grassam, E. H. (1922, revised 1957) *The Beacon Readers* (London: Ginn)

Gray, W. S., Monroe, M., Artley, A. S. & Arbuthnot, M. H. (1956) *The Happy Trio Reading Scheme* (Exeter: Wheaton)

Groff, P. (1980) 'The difference over reading: the gap widens' *Reading,* 14, 1, 14–20

Grundin, H. U. (1980) 'Reading schemes in the infant school' *Reading,* 14, 1, 5–13

Hall, N. A. (1969) *Rescue: A Handbook Of Remedial Reading Techniques For The Classroom Teacher.* Obtainable from Educational Service Inc., PO. Box 219, Stevensville, Michigan 49127, USA

Harris, A. J. & Sipay, E. R. (1975) (6th edition) *How to Increase Reading Ability* (New York: David McKay)

Harris, T. L. & Hodges, R. E. (1981) *A Dictionary of Reading and Related Terms* (Newark, Delaware, USA International Reading Association)

Herr, S. E. (1961) *Learning Activities for Reading* (Dubuque, Iowa, USA: William C. Brown Company Publishers)

Holdaway, D. (1980) *Independence in Reading* (London: Ashton Scholastics)

Hughes, J. M. (1970) *Aids to Reading* (London: Evans)

Hughes, J. M. (1972) *Phonics and the Teaching of Reading* (London: Evans)

Hughes, J. M. (1979) *Using Phonics* (London: Macmillan)

Jackson, S. (1971) *Get Reading Right* (Glasgow: Gibson)

Mackay, D. & Thompson, B. (1970) *Breakthrough to Literacy* (London: Longman)

McCullagh, S. (1981 – 2nd edition) *One, Two, Three and Away!* (St Albans: Hart-Davis Educational)

McKee, P., Harrison, M. L., McCowen, A., Lehr, E. (1956) *The McKee Readers* (London: Nelson)

McNally, J. & Murray, W. (1962 and 1971) *Key Words to Literacy* (London: Schoolmaster Publishing Company)

Melser, J. (1960) *Read it Yourself Books* (Andover: Methuen Educational)

Merritt, J. (1970) 'The intermediate skills' in Gardner, K. (ed.) *Reading Skills: Theory and Practice* (London: Ward Lock Educational)

Moon, B. & Moon, C. (1981) *Individualised Reading*, Comparative Lists of Selected Books for Young Readers (Reading Centre for the Teaching of Reading, University of Reading)

Moon, C. & Raban, B. (1975) *A Question of Reading*, Organisation of resources for reading in primary schools (London: Ward Lock Educational)

Morris, J. M. (1974) *Language in Action* (London: Macmillan)

Moxon, C. V. A. (1962) *A Remedial Reading Method* (London: Methuen)

Moyle, D. (1972) 'The development of the skills of literacy' in Southgate, V. (ed.) *Literacy at All Levels* (London: Ward Lock Educational)

Moyle, D. (1981) *Language Patterns* (Eastbourne: Holt, Rinehart and · Winston)

Murray, W. (1964) *Key Words Reading Scheme* (Loughborough: Wills and Hepworth)

Obrist, C, (1972) *Time for Sounds*, Books 1-6 (Aylesbury: Ginn)

Obrist, C. & Pickard, P.M. (1976) *Time for Reading*, (London: Ginn)

O'Donnell, M. & Munro, R. (1949) *Janet and John* (Welwyn: Nisbet)

O'Donnell, M. & Munro, R. (1965) *Sounds for Reading* (Welwyn: Nisbet)

Platts, M. E. *et al.* (1960) *SPICE: Suggested Activities to Motivate the Teaching of the Language Arts in the Elementary School*. Obtainable from Educational Service Inc., PO Box 219, Stevensville, Michigan 49127, USA

Pumfrey, P. D. (1976) *Reading: Tests and Assessment Techniques* (London: Hodder and Stoughton)

Randell, B. & McDonald, J. (1968) *Methuen Caption Books* (London: Methuen)

Reid, J. & Donaldson, M. (1978–80) *Letter-Link Kits 1–3* (Edinburgh: Holmes McDougall)

Reid, J. & Low, J. (1973) *Link-Up*, Reading Programme (Edinburgh: Holmes McDougall)

Reis, M. (1962) *Fun with Phonics* (Cambridge: Cambridge Art Publishers)

Robinson, H. A. (1972) 'Psycholinguistic inferences for reading instruction' in Southgate, V. (ed.) *Literacy at All Levels* (London: Ward Lock Educational)

Root, B. (1982) *40 Reading Games to Make and Play* (London: Macmillan Education)

Root, B. (1982) *Resources for Teaching Phonics: Annotated Lists of Games, Tests, Tapes, Books and Teaching Aids* (Reading: Centre for the Teaching of Reading, University of Reading)

Russell, D. H. & Karp, E. E. (1959) *Reading Aids through the Grades* (New York: Bureau of Publications, Teachers College, Columbia University)

Schonell, F. J. (1948) *Graded Word Reading Test* (London: Oliver and Boyd)

Schonell, F. J. & Serjeant, I (1939) *Happy Venture Readers* (Edinburgh: Oliver and Boyd)

Simpson, M. (1966) *Ready to Read Scheme* (London: Methuen)

Smith, F. (1971) *Understanding Reading* (New York: Holt, Rinehart and Winston)

Smith, F. (1973) *Psycholinguistics and Reading* (New York: Holt, Rinehart and Winston)

Smith, F. (1978) *Reading* (Cambridge: Cambridge University Press)

Smith, F. (1979) *Reading without Nonsense* (New York: Teachers College Press)

Smith, F. (1980) 'The language arts in the reader's mind' in Bray, G. & Pugh, H. (eds.) 1980 *The Reading Connection* (London: Ward Lock Educational)

Smith, F. (1982) 'What shall we teach when we teach reading?' in Hendry, A. (ed.) 1982 *Teaching Reading: The Key Issues* (London: Heinemann Eucational)

Southgate, V. (1968) *First Words*, Books 1–12 (London: Macmillan)

Southgate, V. (ed.) (1972) *Literacy at All Levels* (London: Ward Lock Educational)

Southgate, V. (ed.) (1982) *Star Series* (London: Macmillan Education)

Southgate, V. (1983) *Children who do read*, Book 1 in the series 'Planning For Reading Success' (Basingstoke: Macmillan Education)

Southgate, V., Arnold, H. & Johnson, S. (1981) *Extending Beginning Reading* (London: Heinemann Educational for the Schools Council)

Southgate, V. and Havenhand, J. (1959) *Sounds and Words*, Books 1–6 and Teachers' Manual (London: Hodder and Stoughton)

Spache, E. B. (1972) *Reading Activities for Child Involvement* (Boston: Allyn and Bacon)

Stott, D. H. (1962) *Programmed Reading Kit* (Glasgow: Holmes McDougall)

Stott, D. H. (1964) *Roads to Literacy* (Glasgow: Holmes McDougall)

Tansley, A. E. (1961) *Sound Sense* (Leeds: Arnold)

Tansley, A. E. (1972) *Reading and Remedial Reading* (London: Routledge and Kegan Paul)

Taylor, J. & Ingleby, T. (1960) *Let's Learn to Read* (London: Blackie)

Taylor, J. & Ingleby, T. (1965) *This is the Way I Go* (London: Longman)

Williams, P., Congdon, P. J., Holder, M. & Sims, N. (1971) *Swansea Test of Phonic Skills* (Oxford: Basil Blackwell)

Webster, J. (1965) *Practical Reading: Some New Remedial Techniques* (London: Evans)

Index

Note: Page-numbers in italics refer to figures.